How to Beat the Australians

Richard Beard is the author of four novels, *X20*, *Damascus*, *The Cartoonist*, *Dry Bones* and one other work of non-fiction, *Muddied Oafs*.

BY THE SAME AUTHOR

Fiction
X 20: A Novel of (Not) Smoking
Damascus
The Cartoonist
Dry Bones

Non-fiction
Muddied Oafs: The Last Days of Rugger

How to Beat the Australians

Richard Beard

YELLOW JERSEY PRESS
LONDON

Published by Yellow Jersey Press 2007

2 4 6 8 10 9 7 5 3 1

First published in Great Britain in 2006 as *Manly Pursuits* by Yellow Jersey Press

Yellow Jersey Press
Random House, 20 Vauxhall Bridge Road,
London SW1V 2SA

Addresses for companies within The Random House Group Limited can be found at: www.randomhouse.co.uk/offices.htm

The Random House Group Limited Reg. No. 954009

www.randomhouse.co.uk

A CIP catalogue record for this book
is available from the British Library

ISBN 9780224075121

Papers used by Random House are natural, recyclable products made from wood grown in sustainable forests. The manufacturing processes conform to the environmental regulations of the country of origin

Typeset by SX Composing DTP, Rayleigh, Essex
Printed and bound in the UK by CPI Bookmarque, Croydon CR0 4TD

To the many who have suffered while the few
embraced defeat and disaster.
England v Australia 1989–2007

Contents

England Collapse

The idea that Englishmen are made of paste, whereas the Australian, native or thoroughly acclimatised, is steel all through, I found to be universal.

Anthony Trollope, *Australia and New Zealand*, 1873

Aged eight, I fell in love with the 1975 England cricket team. That summer, for days on end on BBC1, there assembled a band of unlikely English heroes led by Tony Greig, with his drainpipe trousers and his gum and the upturned peak on his dark blue cap. There was white-haired and nuggety David Steele, Knotty the gnome and his grubby bat, the opener John Edrich with combed eyebrows and sleeves impeccably rolled.

We lost the Ashes. There were any number of reasons, but among them was the Australian change bowler Gary Gilmour, who took 6 for 85 at Headingley. His career was not, however, to blossom – after one more Test against England in Melbourne, he never played for Australia again.

Which was hardly surprising, I thought, since in July 1976 he travelled to the United States and shot dead a

Mormon motel manager in Provo, Utah. Australian to the end, a battler in his baggy green cap, he fronted up to the Utah state marshal and refused to appeal against the death penalty. Instead he quoted Nietzsche, the godfather of sport philosophy – 'a time comes when a man should rise to meet the occasion' – no doubt remembering with scorn the frailty of the English middle order at Leeds.

In January 1977, still in his whites, Gilmour was blindfolded and stood against a post. He was then shot in the heart by a firing squad of volunteer National Guardsmen.

At that time, at that age, an eavesdropper on world events, the difference between Gary Gilmour, Australian medium-fast left-arm swing bowler, and Gary Gilmore, American felon and death-row celebrity, had succeeded in escaping me. But when Greg Chappell's Australians arrived for the next Ashes battle in the summer of '77, the batsmen and bowlers all looked like bandits to me. They had the stubble and the desperado moustaches, and flaunted their ignorance of right from wrong by sledging Derek Randall.

Execution? Too good for the lot of them.

This attitude owes much to the era in which I grew up. My most fertile years for hero worship, between the ages of about seven and fourteen, coincided with the England football team twice failing to qualify for the World Cup finals, in 1974 and 1978. This meant that a generation of sports-mad English children missed out completely on the world's biggest sporting festival.

When we did eventually make it, to Spain in 1982, Kevin Keegan fluffed an easy header to get England out of the group stages, and we might as well not have bothered.

There was no Rugby World Cup, either, and in any case England wouldn't have won it because the players were fat and amateur, and trained on a diet of aftershave.

This left the Ashes. It was the only regular world-class team event in which an English team was guaranteed to feature, and it was world class because England and Australia said so. During this period both countries were routinely thumped by the West Indies, but the intensity of an Ashes summer could obscure the inconvenience of reality. Even better, England won more often than they lost.

Which made Australia's outright cricketing dominance, when it started in 1989, even harder to stomach. By 1998, Australia could comfortably win a five-day Test match against England in two and a half days. In consecutive series, 2001 and 2002/3, the Ashes was over as a contest in the shortest imaginable time, before the end of the third day of the third Test. In the 2006 series, we were subdued from the first wide of the very first day, and yet again surrendered before Christmas.

Worse still, it's impossible for anyone interested in sport to ignore the way Australia's supremacy has crept well beyond the boundaries of cricket. The Australian Lleyton Hewitt is and will always be a Wimbledon champion, whereas Tim Henman will always have his family. Australia has triumphed in two Rugby World Cups, consecutive Cricket World Cups, and the Davis Cup. In the 1990s, they were world champions in twelve team and twenty-one individual sports, a period we in England spent waiting for the nation to be saved by Graeme Hick.

There isn't even the sweet and sour consolation of thinking they save their best for England. At the 2004 Athens Olympics, Australia won more medals than all but three other countries – the United States, China and Russia. These medals were distributed across fifteen sports, a range matched only by the United States, and there were no medals for rugby league. The Australians might also have been in with a shout at Olympic Australian Rules.

Suddenly no event anywhere in the world was safe, and at the 2002 Winter Olympics Stephen Bradbury won gold in short track speed skating, not a popular hobby on the beaches of Queensland. It's true that the other four finalists wiped out in a mass collision, and the same thing had happened to Bradbury in his semi-final. But you've got to be in it to win it, and the green and gold is always in it.

They have world champions in motorcycling, aerial skiing, eight-ball pool and orienteering. There was an Australian, Luc Longley, making rebounds alongside Michael Jordan in his luminary years for the Chicago Bulls; Australians riddle the US baseball leagues; they kick field goals in the NFL. They have a dozen riders in the Tour de France while until recently we had only one, David Millar, who was caught taking drugs. He couldn't even beat the testers properly, in cycling a minimum competitive requirement.

I don't know how the French feel about being beaten by Australians in their national sport. I do know that as a basic rule of engagement, speaking for myself, I enjoy Australia's athletes losing in any sport, to any opposition, at any time. This is what it means, in Anglo-Australian relations, to be right-minded, and in twenty years as an active adult sportsman I haven't met a single Australian who could persuade me otherwise.

And I've met Australians. It's almost impossible, if you like playing games as much as I do, to avoid them. The winters aren't so bad; whenever a cocky twenty-year-old from the southern hemisphere makes a difference in a game of rugby, whether I'm playing in Paris or Nailsea or Chiba City, I can convince myself (whatever anyone says) that he must have come from New Zealand. Summers are trickier. If you play social cricket in London, anywhere from Battersea to Hampstead, an Australian ringer can be expected to ruin your day.

My cricket team's oldest fixture, first played in 1989, once looked like evolving nicely into a keen annual derby. Our team is full of natural sportsmen who've never played much cricket. The other lot used to have keen cricketers with no talent. This meant that in the early days we would usually win. Then the other side organised winter nets; they improved a little every year and we aged a little every year, but just as talent and practice began to even each other out, the Australians came.

They were young, they were backing themselves, and they were doing most of the batting and bowling for the enemy.

The first time was at Parliament Hill, on one of the municipal pitches squeezed between care-in-the-community picnics and games of touch rugby. The other side had only ten players, and lost their last batter still twenty-three runs short of the target we'd set them. Another well-earned victory, or so I thought, but our celebrations were cut short by a new batsman striding to the wicket, a mysterious number eleven. Padded up, he was sweaty from playing touch rugby, but it was only one man, and not even a cricketer. He was offered guard. 'Nah, mate,' he said, bat aloft, flexing his knees, hitching up the box inside his rugby shorts. 'No worries.'

Only one Australian.

He stood there and hit sixteen runs, then a single. From the other end he hit a six.

Ever since (every year a loss apart from one solitary, almost glorious tie) we first count the Australians as a way of gauging how long the match might last, and then accept, in despair, that there is only the one remedy: recruit some Australians of our own, if we're serious about winning, and hope our Australians are better than their Australians.

It hurts the worst in cricket because cricket isn't decided by brawn. We can't simply shrug and tell ourselves Australians eat more meat as children. Or more children as meat. I'd believe anything, especially after living every slight of the longest losing streak in Ashes history, and then having that rubbed in by part-time London barmen whose birthright is to bowl vicious inswinging leg-cutters.

To an Englishman, too often on the losing side, Australia can seem sports-mad, sports-drunk, as if a passion for games must be intrinsic to the business of being Australian. How else to explain their supremacy? Don't they ever get distracted by anything else?

I don't know. I've never been there.

In the golden age of England versus Australia, when I was young and we didn't always lose, Australian history was whatever had happened in the last Test match. Despite Gary Gilmour's delinquent double life, I doubt I was aware of the unique history of transportation sometimes paraded to explain Australia's sharp competitive instinct. In its most basic form, this is the theory that Australians, given their convict ancestry, are difficult to beat at games because they're the toughest bastards on earth.

In *The Fatal Shore*, his epic history of the penal system in Australia, Robert Hughes writes that 'transportation did rid England of many real sociopaths, men whose aggression and violence were built into their genetic labyrinth', and he didn't necessarily mean the convicts. The New South Wales Corps took a little too much pleasure in the cat, with its nine leather tails, each one knotted seven times and tipped with wire. At first, the marines strapped convicts to trees. Then the sane, law-abiding soldiers of the British armed forces invented the triangle, a tripod of wooden beams. The military men could now alternate between watching flesh peel off a prisoner's back, and observing the finer expressions of pain on his face, much more satisfactory and even comparatively interesting.

Official punishment records show that floggable crimes in the early colony included a hundred lashes for saying 'Oh my God', and another hundred for 'Singing a Song'. If that song was 'Aussie Aussie Aussie, oi oi oi' then the lashes were justifiably doubled. A prisoner could be flogged for losing his shoelaces or waving a twig, and flogging wasn't a short sharp shock. It lasted longer than that. The doctor and commandant made it a habit to walk a hundred yards between each of the hundred lashes, dragging out the punishment to about ninety minutes, or roughly the length of a football match. The convicts endured. A hundred lashes or until their boots filled with blood, whichever came sooner.

The idea that Australia's unforgiving past still counts for something is a notion beloved of the less complicated type of Englishman, like idiot-king Ian Botham. In Australia in 1991, Botham called his hosts 'descendants of convicts' and then, as a sideshow to the action between wickets (England drubbed 3–0 for the Ashes), the England team held up their wrists to the crowd in a mime, as if manacled.

This barminess is now perpetuated by the barmy army, who like to chant, 'You're just a bunch of convicts.' This has about as much truth and sense in it as another favourite song kept in reserve for Australians, 'Sheepshagger, la la la'. The first line goes 'Sheepshagger, la la la'. The second line goes 'Sheepshagger, la la la'. The third line goes . . . And so on, until the end of lager and time.

At least Botham and the barmy army demonstrate that English people of all backgrounds can be objectionable, and not just the toffs. They jeer at an idea of the stereotyped Australian, but in the early days of Australia we were careful to keep alive some favoured stereotypes of our own. Whenever the ruling class risked being seen as anything but effete bumblers, we used to send out administrators with names of the calibre of Sir John Eardley Eardley-Wilmot, no further qualifications required. Sir John stepped off the boat dangling a baronet's handkerchief at a time when early Australians would discourage a dobber – an informer – by biting his nose and ears off. This was a retribution commonly known as 'taking the dog's muzzle'.

And that's not cricket.

It's tempting to short-circuit these perceptions. The English bat with embroidered handkerchiefs, whereas a physically robust past and persistent clumsiness with knife and fork is somehow rewarded in Australians by obduracy in tight sporting situations. There's also the hunger. Those sentenced to Parts Beyond the Seas had often been reprieved from hanging. They were offered a second chance, and the determinist theory has it that Australians will therefore grasp sporting (and other) opportunities immediately they arise.

Whatever their precise motivation, it's true that Australians quickly found the sport in transportation. Below decks they ripped the pages out of Bibles and made playing cards, using soot for the black suits, and blood for red. In Sydney they immediately organised prizefights, and although the first hundred horses only arrived in Australia in 1798, by 1810 there was a throughbred race meeting in Sydney's Hyde Park.

But these were habits of life shared with England. With an equal passion for fighting and racing, the eighteenth-century English were also tough bastards, the wayward parents of Wellington's 'scum of the earth'. Out in the counties we even played cricket for several centuries without pads.

If these facts had any relevance to sporting contests today, nearly every nineteenth-century headcase would have needed to be shipped to Australia. Unlikely. One estimate has it that in 1797 one Londoner in eight was living off crime. That's a lot of tough nuts left behind (assuming crooks are tough) and their descendants in England should be as likely as any Australian to take a match-winning risk on the morning of the fifth and deciding day.

And if Australian sporting success could be explained by genetic inheritance, their achievements would stop at the racecourse. Thanks to the immaculate records of the British Empire, we know that the majority of transported convicts measured between 5 foot 3 and 5 foot 8 inches tall. On the new continent an improved diet made their children taller, and their children's children taller again.

Horse jockeys became opening bowlers and lock forwards and oarsmen, and it wasn't just physique that was changed by the opportunity of Australia. Attitudes could shift and develop just as dramatically, until the common national denominator is unlikely to have become anything as straightforward as the simple will to win.

Australia's convict history is an insignificant factor in the nation's status as a sporting superpower. During the full period of transportation, from 1788 to 1868, about 160,000 prisoners arrived in Australia. In 1851, after gold was discovered near Melbourne, twice that number of free men arrived in a single year, and they weren't all the type to bite a man's nose off, or open the Australian bowling.

Convicts against the mother country makes arresting copy for sports reporters when the clock nears quarter past five, but it's a lazy and irrelevant connection, and has been for a long time. Even at the end of the nineteenth century, you didn't call Australian sportsmen or Australian crowds sons of convicts. If you did, as the English cricketers Emmett and Ulyett found out at the Sydney Cricket Ground in 1879, you'd be criminally assaulted.

The feeling lingers, however, that Australian and English sportspeople are somehow differently equipped. If the rivalry is gladiatorial, then it doesn't seem as evenly matched as the shield and short sword against the trident and net. The Australians have the sword *and* the trident, and in recent years we've backed off, fending and feinting, knowing the result in advance but hoping at best to make a fight of it. If this difference has little to do with convict blood, then what exactly causes it?

A convict heritage was once known in Australia as the Taint, or even more sensationally, the Stain, indelible and passed down through generations like an embarrassing mattress. When this notion faded, it was replaced by a more complicated feeling that A.A. Phillips in 1966 famously described as the Cultural Cringe. This was the inferiority that Australians supposedly felt when comparing European culture and society to their own. The Cringe came in two forms, according to Phillips: the Cringe Direct and the Cringe Inverted. The Cringe Direct was university students contriving human Union Jacks for visits by the Royal Shakespeare Company. Inverted, it became the ocker Australian male flaunting his assumed grossness of character, mostly in relation to sport, beer-drinking and women:

'What does an Australian cricketer say to a feminist with no arms and no legs?'

'Nice tits. I'll get my own tinny.'

Australian sporting victories were supposed to help banish such feelings of inadequacy, and perhaps they did. In the popular mythology, Bradman's batting and batting and batting in England in 1934 was followed avidly by families gathered round the wireless from Darwin to Hobart. The Australian people were appreciating some unique and superior quality invested in a fellow Australian, or as Thomas Keneally later wrote, 'While no Australian had written *Paradise Lost*, Don Bradman had made a hundred before lunch at Lord's' – an achievement by implication far beyond the abilities of poet John Milton, who was blind.

After Bradman came Betty Cuthbert, Dawn Fraser, Herb Elliot, Rod Laver; these were the battling culture heroes who by defying all odds to win across the globe gradually fostered a sense of shared Australianness.

Once, this may well have been true, but it's not a picture

of Australia I recognise. *I'm* the one who's always felt inadequate and second rate, and in need of a victory, and if you've ever woken up to *Test Match Special* and groaned at the morning scorecard from the Gabba, you'll know what I mean.

Or if you've ever played cricket in London. In 2004, against my ageing and tiring bowling attack, a hungover Australian ringer hit fifty, vomited at the side of the wicket, wiped his mouth on his batting glove, vomited again, belched, and then hit another fifty, all while I stood at long off moving fielders to the boundary and trying to identify how, exactly, he could be said to be cringing before me.

To my generation the Cultural Cringe is invisible to the naked eye: Australia is patently superior. I know this because each stage of my upbringing has featured patently superior Australians. As part of our teatime television diet, just home from school, we watched full-colour underwater Australians saving the oceans on *Barrier Reef*. They had aqualungs and miniature submarines; we had holes in the top right-hand corner of our dented desks for inkwells. In the holidays there was the all-summer knockabout double act of Thomson and Lillee on BBC1 (highlights BBC2), followed in the '80s by late-night Clive James, the funniest man on Channel 4. Later, at college, there was Germaine Greer, the world's most feminist feminist, only offset by lunchtime *Neighbours*, reminding us in our cold student rooms that every home in Melbourne has a sunny garden with swimming pool. For the rest of my days I'll be haunted by the knowledge that Kylie Minogue was the second-best-looking girl on the average Australian Ramsay Street. They gave us Kylie, but they kept the gorgeous Plain Jane Superbrain for themselves.

Here's an indicator of changing times. In 1951 the Australian football team was beaten at home 17–0 by England. 17–0. No wonder they used to cringe. In 2003 at Upton Park, where balls were being kicked since before the idea of Canberra, England were humbled 3–1 by the rampant Socceroos. At that match the Australians in the crowd chanted, 'You'll never win the Ashes,' and I believed them. They also held up a banner saying, 'If we win, you suck at everything.' The Cringe had swung so far across the hemispheres that I didn't take this banner to refer exclusively to sport. It meant we sucked at TV presenting and feminist critiques and literary novels and female impersonators and daytime television soap operas. We sucked at getting out of bed in the morning, at pulling our socks on, at making tea. We lost at football to Australia; truly, we sucked at everything.

The Australian Cultural Cringe had disappeared, to be replaced, on the English side, by a new and chronic condition. The Recreational Cringe. That's what it was, that's what we had. And personally I had it bad.

Often it came in the direct form – through the 1990s we just had to hold up our hands and admit that Australians were better at sport than we were. We sent out Commons select committees to find out why, and they came back tanned and happy and said it was the weather. It also came Inverted, with jokes about English cricket a growing sector of the nation's comic stock:

'Doctor, doctor, I can't score runs, I'm a terrible bowler and I can't hold a catch. What should I do?'

'Have you ever considered giving up cricket?'

'I can't. I'm playing for England tomorrow.'

The Recreational Cringe spored and spread, seeding itself widely at a time when leisure could matter more than culture. England and Australia had changed places, and the roles were reversed. We were inadequate. They were sporting winners and had what we wanted.

At the end of England's disastrous Ashes tour to Australia in 2003, Christopher Martin-Jenkins headlined his concluding report for *The Times*: STRENGTH OF CHARACTER HOLDS KEY TO AUSTRALIA'S DOMINANCE. The Cringe had become so entrenched it seemed reasonable to reach this vast conclusion from so simple an argument as sport, as games.

Later the same year, however, there came a ray of light, an event to suggest the Cringe might yet be overcome. England had won the 2003 Rugby World Cup, in Australia, against the Australians, in a thrilling contest that only the toughest, most cussed side would win. For once, that was us. Admittedly, on that occasion English dominance lasted precisely eighty-one minutes. This is the pitch time between Jonny Wilkinson's last-minute drop goal and our next defeat by the Wallabies.

Neverthless, the rugby team had proved that beating Australians was possible, and as their all-conquering cricketers prepared to land in England in the summer of 2005, set on defending the Ashes for a record eighth time, I found I couldn't sit still. Ahead of me was the horrific prospect of Christopher Martin-Jenkins judging the weakness of my character, months of Sunday cricket in London being bashed by Australian bar staff, and the possibility of another faded summer to that familiar headline refrain: ENGLAND COLLAPSE. I wanted to uncurl from the Cringe, look up, stretch out my arms and stop feeling inferior. I'd had enough of the decadence of the English athlete. I was truly fed up.

Fired up like this, fully motivated in the face of the old

enemy, I was then brutally overlooked by the selectors. They failed to pick me for England, and not for the first time, either. In a blaze of unEnglish bravado, of almost Australian strength of character and conviction, I therefore decided to select myself, to prove once and for all to my own satisfaction that Englishmen were not made of paste.

It was now or never to go and beat the Australians.

First Test

In England, the obsession with sport is bad enough, but even fiercer passions are aroused in young countries where games-playing and nationalism are both recent developments.

George Orwell, 'The Sporting Spirit', 1945

On the plane they hand out landing cards and Option A is 'Migrating Permanently to Australia'. Steady on, I think. 'Is This Your First Visit?'

Yes, it is, but not my first attempt.

In the back garden in Swindon we used to dig for it. If the hole was ever dug deep enough, we would of course come out on the other side of the world, in Australia. This was just another piece of adult misinformation. No matter how long you dig you're never going to make it. Look at a globe. If you start from Swindon, and keep digging straight down, you'll eventually come out somewhere in the Pacific Ocean. But we didn't look at a globe, and anyway we were English so we gave up long before we got there and came inside for tea.

After a journey through the earth's core we'd have

kicked ourselves for missing it, especially given the size of the place. At the time, of course, we expected to know we'd arrived because our heads would pop up in a desert of red rocks and kangaroos. This version of the outback is shorthand for real Australia: it's what tourists usually want to see, and in his masterpiece novel *Voss*, Patrick White assembles a foreign-led expedition with a shared and acknowledged vice – 'the insatiable desire for perpetual motion through the unpleasanter portions of Australia'.

This is not a vice I share. I want to stay where the people are, where they gather together for sport. I therefore take a minibus from Sydney airport into the city. It's a bright midwinter day, about twenty-three degrees, and I'm fascinated by everything, even air cargo containers stacked on a ridge against the blue of the sky.

I'm reminded of other boys' houses when I was a child. They were the same but different, strange but familiar, and at first Australia has the same kind of feel. I've seen the country on television, imagined it, feared it, yelled at its sportspeople, but had no real proof it existed. It might have been a *Neighbours* set, but in fact here it is, like an inexact drawing. It resembles what I know from England, but the houses need more detail and the cars and trees are slightly wrong.

Like the season. For me this is summer, and the warmth of Sydney feels like summertime, the cricket season, but I won't be beating the Australians at cricket because here they insist it's winter. This probably explains the emptiness of the bus, just me and the Samoan driver, and I ask him about a line painted on the road, a mesmerising and apparently random blue traffic line that slices from one carriageway to the other, taking the shortest possible route at roundabouts.

It's the Olympic marathon route, patchy where it flits across the tarmac, bright where it aligns with the curb, here and for the next twenty-six miles. Sydney suddenly seems a big place, where you can run marathons without leaving the city, and as I look out the window at Australians going about their business in Surry Hills or outside the shops on Oxford Street, it's hard to believe I can beat them all. I can barely find it in my heart to *dislike* them all, because it's not true that I bow to no one in my frustration with sporting Australians. I do bow down. I bow to Douglas Jardine, the Scottish England cricket captain on the 1932 bodyline tour.

To Jardine, beating the Australians meant everything, and tour manager 'Plum' Warner later wrote that Jardine's 'general dislike of Australians was almost pathological'. Jardine insisted that the Australian cricket team be known collectively as bastards, with the exception of Donald Bradman. Out of respect for Bradman's astonishing performances against England in 1930, and to distinguish him from the rest of the team, Bradman would be known as the *little* bastard. Jardine, not surprisingly, was called a bastard straight back by an Australian player out on the pitch. He made a formal complaint, which led the Australian captain to round his team up, in front of Jardine, and demand, 'Which one of you bastards called this bastard a bastard?'

Jardine was incorruptible, implacable, and continued bowling to kill even when the series was dead. 'Douglas Jardine is loathed,' wrote Old Etonian 'Gubby' Allen on his captain, 'he is a perfect swine and I can think of no words fit for Mummy to see when I describe him.' These days, we'd call him a winner, but that still doesn't make him particularly nice, or any more palatable to the Mummy country.

This is one of the paradoxes of sport. We want to win; we want our heroes to win. But we also want to preserve our faith in sport as a vehicle for social cohesion and moral improvement. Or at least I do, because I'm a believer, but it's clearly not working if you want to win as badly as Jardine or the Australians (and I'm thinking of the Chappell brothers and Allan Border and Steve Waugh, cricketers so gritty that lunch is sandwiches with sand in).

It's not good to want to win so badly, and I want to win against Australians to make this point. Only I'll have to do it on my own. It feels dishonest to surround myself with a team of Australians to beat other Australians. So team sports aside, I'll take them on at anything, not at the elite level but at a lower level, at my level. I'm going to front up, have a go in the country where a fair go for everyone is a founding principle of the value system. I'll find out how and why they win, and whether it does them any good.

In my favour, seeing as I haven't come all this way to lose, I've an eye for a ball and a competitive instinct undimmed since I first took twenty wickets in an Ashes Test aged six. I also have a fair idea of the kind of Australians I need to beat.

I therefore climb off the bus at Circular Quay, and head for the waterfront and the ferries. I'm in the right place: my ferry is green and gold, and considerately it makes a point of running out past the Harbour Bridge and the gleaming Opera House. I'm in Australia, in Sydney, on the outside deck of a Sydney Harbour ferry.

I'm making my way to Manly.

A flying boat glints overhead, and we chug towards the

Heads, as far as the ocean gap. As the ferry turns, exposed to the ocean for about a minute, it lurches in a wider, wilder swell, but before the fat-bottomed boat has to cope with the full implications of the Pacific it's under the lee of North Head, and puffing jauntily up towards Manly Wharf. White brochure blocks of flats dazzle the shoreline and anchored sailboats in Manly Cove bob and point, submitting to the wind, eager to show they know their place. The placid wharfside beaches are raked and clean.

Manly isn't all Australia, I appreciate that, and if I'd gone somewhere else, things may well have turned out differently. In the town of Daydream in Queensland, for example, I may have met less competitive Australians. Or in the state of Victoria I could have risked my life at Indented Head. But I had to start somewhere, and I decided on the Sydney coastal suburb of Manly (pop. 37,000), seven miles north of the Opera House, a peninsula of land squeezed narrow by the ocean, pinched on both sides by clear blue water.

D.H. Lawrence has his characters come to Manly in the novel *Kangaroo*. Of course he does, and he describes Manly as 'like a bit of Margate with sea-side shops and restaurants', an unlikely comparison that had seemed just one consequence of writing 150,000 words of novel in five weeks. But no, Lawrence has a point. Immediately opposite the ferry terminal is the Corso, Manly's main pedestrian shopping street. It is instantly recognisable as a precinct of the wandering territory of Touristland.

Manly Corso is shouty with the plastic and cotton factory wrack stacked up high wherever tourists don't qualify as people: they're visitors. It's not as if they're coming back. There are bush hats with dangling plastic corks, Manly Beach beach towels, and Barcelona and

Arsenal football jerseys at ten dollars each. There are four chip shops. One is new, one has been there a while, a third is a health hazard, and the fourth is sealed off by hardboard and graffiti – *Freemasons Out*. This will soon be the new one, because Touristland has its repeating rituals like anywhere else – aim to get your chips from whichever shop is currently in second place.

Then, just like Lawrence, at the far end of the Corso I'm stunned out of comparisons with anywhere else on earth. I gawk at the glory of the Pacific, 'rolling in on the yellow sand: the wide fierce sea, that makes all the built-over land dwindle into non-existence'.

Lawrence is brilliant on the liquid Pacific – the 'heavy, earth-despising swell', the 'star-white foam' – but I'm soon distracted by the people. Every person on the promenade, including young mothers and layabouts and council sweepers in fluorescent waistcoats, is wearing wraparound shades. This makes it seem as if everyone would prefer to conceal their identity, is actually a gangster or sports celebrity merely taking a break to sip at a takeaway cappuccino, watch the power-walkers and power-prammers power on by, gaze at the beach, the incoming sea.

I've rented a unit about halfway along Manly Beach, but with enough streets and buildings between me and the ocean to keep down the cost. It turns out that the Corso is a strip of tourist tat sandwiched between two more genteel residential areas. To the south, on the hill up to North Head, the square sandstone tower of St Patrick's College is the dominant feature overlooking the beach. In my direction, the low roofs of beach Australia are flat against the clear winter sky.

* * *

Bag stowed. Door locked. I'm back outside in the Australian sunshine and I'm ready. Now I just have to decide at what sport to beat the Australians *first*.

Since I stopped playing rugby, I've been looking for a game better suited to my age. Not that I've stopped rugby, not exactly, I'm just playing much more slowly, but I wouldn't want Australians to think age is a problem, or an excuse. But when my knees pack up for good, and my fast-twitch muscle refuses to twitch fast, I'll be looking for something gentler to do with my Saturday afternoons.

I suck in the ocean air, puff out my chest. I'm feeling up to the challenge of Manly lawn bowls. I therefore head back towards the Corso, because the Bowls Club is on the milder, harbour side of Manly, beyond the tennis courts and the Oval. Manly Oval is the local ground for grade cricket in the summer, and in the winter the square grows over and it's home to the Manly Marlins rugby club. It's a midweek afternoon, but there's a game on, and I can't resist going in for my first sight of Australian sport on its own turf.

It's an Ashes match. King's School Worcester Under 16s rugby team, on their tour of a lifetime, are getting ready for their first game in Australia, against St Paul's School Manly. I wonder if the boys from Worcester are as determined as I am, so I ask them. Inside-centre Jeff Ballard (16) is expecting a tough contest, though he predicts the Australians will be more organised, and, partially, more Samoan. This means bigger, and Jeff seems to be suggesting it makes sense to be frightened. I scoff, and question the English will to win.

'We want to win *a lot*!' he insists. But then adds, 'Our really quick player broke his leg.'

The coach Jonny Mason, not much younger than me and therefore sure to suffer from the Cringe, expects the Manly boys to be physically stronger and naturally fitter. Ah, the direct version. He also mentions the St Paul's headmaster, a man with a sense of occasion, who claimed earlier at lunch that his pupils ate three or four steaks a day.

In the match, the Australian boys look very like the English boys, but with unlimited access to extra-strength Sun-in. And the sun. They also have a more precise understanding of the directional concept known in rugby as forward. They win 50–7, another generation effortlessly asserting their Australian superiority. I'm outraged. As they say in politics, far more often than anything gets done: Something must be done.

Beyond the Oval I size up Manly Bowls Club. An elderly gent is snipping the edges of one of the rinks, and another old gent is practising in full whites and a panama hat. It looks unthreatening enough, a low-intensity arena offering a mild introduction to Manly sport, and it doesn't require three or four steaks a day. I boost myself with the thought that bowls is one of the few games on earth where I can flaunt my physical fitness, because bowling years are like dog years. They use a different scale, and seventy-five to a lawn bowler is about thirty-eight among humans – just over the hill (but only just). In bowling years I'm a whippersnapper, a tyro, a bold young Turk.

I've played before, as it happens, an afternoon of ends with Christine in Plymouth. Because that's where Christine came from, Plymouth, and a game of bowls was an ingenious substitute for conversation. It was also a local homage to Sir Francis Drake, the Ian Botham of the high seas, the stroppy explorer curling a cunning backhand draw shot before saving the nation from the Spanish Armada ('All right then, if I *have* to').

That's how I know that the second great advantage of bowls is that it requires no expert motor skills. Assuming I can manage the lack of expertise, winning and losing becomes solely a question of attitude. I'll be the hard case of Manly Lawn Bowls.

Unless, that is, I'm not.

It's possible that bowls, however leisurely it seems, may immediately reveal stark differences in sporting culture between Australia and England. A classic of the literature, *Fundamentals of Lawn Bowls*, was written by an Australian, Albert Newton, in 1960. Mr Newton offers devilish winning strategies before moving crisply along to the importance of temperament: 'Temperament is just as important in bowls as in any other sport. Many bowlers are top-liners in social matches, but are beaten by inferior opponents in games of importance.' The tone of disappointment here is unmistakable, and Newton won't let this one go. 'The desire for power is as strong in bowls as in anything else,' he concludes, and I'm already beginning to regret my choice of game.

Especially when I try to learn something from a British guide published in 1991, *Flat Green Bowls; The Skills of the Game*, by Gwyn John. This book has little to say about temperament and the will to power, but rather more about arthritis in the bowling hand, especially the wrist and fingers. It also emphasises, early and often, the importance of a 'complete set of waterproof clothing'.

While on one level I approve of these very British priorities, they don't exactly inspire me. I feel unprepared, though the true Brit Mr John does touch proudly on recent advances the home countries have been making in mental preparation: 'Some bowlers like to arrive quite early before a game, and perhaps take a quiet walk around the green.'

That's me, and I take the walk. It doesn't help. I have a vision of Mr Newton and his pals back in the pavilion, staring at each other without blinking and reciting, from memory, *Thus Spake Zarathrustra*.

But the Cringe has to be confronted, and I walk into the low pavilion at the Manly Bowling Club. It has a bar, which is closed. There's no sign of Mr Newton or disciples of Newton, but this is going to be my first indication of whether Australia is a paradise of sport, or just of winning. The popular Australian self-image, as idealised in self-reliant heroes like the bushranger and the digger, depends on a strong sense of egalitarianism and giving everyone a fair go. Mate. I'm about to find out whether I çan get a fair go at community sport in Manly.

In the office I find the Minister of Fun. I know this from the publicity leaflet pinned to the office door. The Manly Bowls Club, installed on this prime piece of Manly real estate for nearly a hundred years, is looking for a saviour, anyone who can resurrect the former popularity of bowls. They've chosen Bruce Malouf, a short fat man who can't stand still, and who isn't a bowler himself. Nevertheless, he claims on flyers and in the *Manly Daily* that he, Bruce Malouf the Minister of Fun, can single-handedly inject some rock 'n' roll into Manly lawn bowls by tempting youngsters on the weekend prowl with the 5 Bs: Bowls Beer Barbecues Barefeet Bonding.

'Are you with a corporate group?' he asks.

'Er, no.'

'We also do bowling as a corporate bonding exercise?'

The rising intonation is hopeful, and then registering my lack of reaction, displeased.

'I was more interested in just bowls.'

He grimaces and shifts his weight as if itching in awkward places he almost dares scratch. For Bruce, bowls is a business venture, not a sport, and therefore doesn't involve a warm sporting welcome. In fact, any kind of welcome. It seems that this is not a Minister of Fun day, and he rushes about the mess of the clubhouse doing nothing much, pretending to be busy as a sign of success. He doesn't know if he can talk to me.

'What do you actually want?'

'I'd like to play bowls. Here at the bowls club. Maybe I could join in with the 5 Bs.'

'You have to come in a group.'

'I don't have a group. I only just arrived.'

'Sorry, can't help, mate. What *do* you want?'

I think what Bruce is trying to say is, 'What's in it for me?'

I have nothing to offer, except the observation that Bruce reminds me of something Martin Amis is supposed to have said, that character is just another word for arsehole. This isn't always true, of course, and inside many a character is a lovely person choked by a cartoon laugh, but it's true often enough to be worth bearing in mind. It's one of those minor life rules that through experience commands respect, like being wary of anything advertised aggressively as fun. The more fun promised, the less likely the delivery.

Bruce eventually, grudgingly, shows me a promotional video for his bowling business, in which the New South Wales Super 12 rugby union team bowl and drink beer to a soundtrack of 'Start Me Up'. I wonder if the young and fit need bowls. Don't they have enough? The trouble with *Rock 'n' Bowl* (that's the name of the product) is that if you're young enough to like rock music and getting pissed, you're young enough to be out playing a proper sport. I want bowls to be old and genteel, like it's supposed to be, otherwise how can I hope to win? I don't want to play singles against Matthew Burke and the Australian rugby team. I don't want to do anything at all to 'Eye of the Tiger'.

I therefore leave the Manly Bowls Club in the hands of unfriendly Bruce Malouf, and because I'm being upbeat and optimistic, keeping the Cringe at a distance, I convince myself that my first encounter in Manly went rather well. I think. I then wait at a bus stop beside the Manly Oval for a bus to take me up the Old Pittwater Road, which links the townships of Sydney's Northern Beaches. Five minutes later, the bus drops me at the gates of North Manly Bowls Club. It's Australia, it's sport; there are 4,500 bowls clubs to choose from, and half a million active bowlers just waiting to be beaten.

Gerry Muoio is waiting for me under the awning of the long, low, sun-faded clubhouse.

'You wanna play *bocce*?'

It seems like another mistake. Gerry is in his mid-sixties and has recently been elected president of North Manly Bowls Club, but he started out as a player of *bocce*, the Italian version of bowls.

'I was hoping to play bowls.'

'Nah, mate. You wanna know about *bocce*.'

'Or maybe bowls? A bit of practice, I thought, and then play a game or two.'

'We have 140 members, a hundred play *bocce*.'

'Must be an interesting game.'

'Shit yeah.'

There are four bowling rinks at North Manly, and each green is a whitish colour, like a perfect five-day cricket pitch. 'So about the bowls?' On Australia Day, Gerry tells me, they have bowls in the morning and *bocce* in the afternoon. He says it as if half and half is only just acceptable as a share-out of the national day.

'I been here since 1958. You wuhneevenborn. Wanna know about *bocce*?'

Gerry is wearing a green sleeveless fleece with *North Manly Bowls Club* embroidered on the chest. His baseball cap says *North Manly Bocce*, and on competition days all bowls players have to wear name tags. It's in the rules. Gerry's partner for an away match later today is sitting in the shade under the overhanging roof. His name tag says *Michaele*, and the two of them quickly make me welcome. This is more like what I had in mind, getting involved directly in Australian sport at junior and local level, away from the glitz and achievement of the elite. Elite sport might impose itself, and have a strong inspirational effect, but it's never the full story.

'You need Frank Geer,' Gerry tells me. 'He's the bowls coach.'

We try to find Frank, but after a few phone calls it turns out that Frank's wife has been admitted to hospital. In other sports, this would mean catastrophes and necessary explanations, instant sympathy and possibly a whip-round. In bowls, it's apparently not such an unusual reason for missing a day on the rinks.

'Frank'll fix you up,' Gerry says. He eyes me carefully. I stare back at him, and win, so he doesn't say whatever it was he was about to say about *bocce*.

'And when I come back,' I say, 'after I've tried out bowls, let's have a game of *bocce*.'

'Shit yeah.'

This isn't turning out as I'd hoped. I wait outside the bowls club for a while, and watch as buses marked '000 Special' pass me by. They're special because they're empty and they never stop. I eventually give up waiting and trudge back down the Pittwater Road towards Manly. I'm not sure what exactly I'd expected, but the Recreational Cringe presupposes an unrealistic view of Australian sportspeople, supermen like Reg 'Snowy' Baker, born 1884 in Darlinghurst, Sydney.

Snowy was a champion in twenty-six sports, including pegging tents and wrestling on horseback. In 1904 he played rugby union against England, and in 1908 competed at the London Olympics as a swimmer and springboard diver. With time on his hands, he also fought for the Olympic middleweight boxing title against J.W.H.T. Douglas, representing England. With the judges split, the gold medal was awarded to Douglas by the referee, also a Mr Douglas, primarily because he was J.W.H.T.'s father. Snowy solved the refereeing problem when he ran into the younger Douglas a few days later at the National Sporting Club. They removed their dinner jackets and fought bare-knuckle. The Australian won by a knockout.

After that he set swimming records in Denmark, won water polo matches in Finland and Holland, and gave exhibitions of diving and wrestling in Sweden and Germany. He standardised the weight categories in boxing, a reform adopted in the US and now universally accepted. He starred in two Hollywood films as Jack Airlie, Australian special agent, and then taught Douglas Fairbanks how to ride horses and crack whips for *Son of Zorro*.

Snowy Baker is the least I expect from the standard Australian competitor – Brett Lee with a whip. It therefore makes no sense to take them on one-to-one, man-to-man, despite what I thought when I arrived. That's asking for trouble, unarmed, especially with the spectre of Gary Gilmour, cricket shirt punctured with bloody holes in the heart region, laughing down at me from the great Australian pantheon in the sky. I need to approach this less directly, or lay hands on some weaponry of my own. Or both.

The next day, I'm collected at a street corner by the captain of the Manly Small Bore Rifle Club. Her name is Maria Silva.

'Welcome to Australia,' she says, beaming a smile and leaning over to open the door of her 4x4. 'Welcome to Manly.'

The Manly Small Bore Rifle Club is open every Wednesday and Saturday, and many local residents don't know it's there, tucked in by the creek behind Nolan Reserve where kids make the most of the sunshine playing soccer, kicking a rugby ball, plain larking about.

Inside the wooden clubhouse it's freezing. This is good. The feel of an English winter cancels out local advantage. The clubhouse was built in 1941, and not much has been done to it since. It's a large open room and looks like a scout hut, with bench tables and a long wall-mounted blackboard recording many Saturdays of scores. Fading signs in English, French and German tell the post-war Manly shooter to point the gun at the target when it's loaded – '*das Gewehr Muss an der Schulter Anliegen*'. This is the only German in sight, whereas when I was last shooting, as a twelve-year-old schoolboy, imaginary Germans were everywhere, which was why we were armed to the teeth and filling them full of lead. The target was merely a guide.

'It's not much, eh?' Maria says, pointing to a table where I can put down her gun case. 'The council wants to knock it down and build a netball centre.'

'Is that right?'

'That's what we hear.'

But first they'll have to deal with Maria Silva, a 4-foot-8-inch killing machine with aviator sunglasses and a jangle of silver chains at her neck. I'm confident I could beat her at wrestling, unless it was on horseback. At shooting I'm not so sure, because this is unfamiliar territory. The sports I know well, usually played outside with a ball, celebrate strength, fitness and skill. But as Americans once liked to say, God made the Colt 45 to even things up.

Maria is Angolan Portuguese, and in 1975 was at university in the capital Luanda when war broke out. She arrived in Lisbon as a refugee, but decided Portugal was too cold and emigrated to Australia in 1987. Now she's the captain, acting treasurer and statistician of the Manly Small Bore Rifle Club.

'It was in the family, mate. My mum and dad used to take me out for the zebra, buffalo, impala. Yeah, that's right. They move, they get shot!'

Maria has a silver laugh, spilling straight from the melting pot. It's as if she genuinely can't believe her luck, as happy as ingots to be alive.

'You gotta laugh,' she says, one of her favourite expressions, but instead of laughing I stand absolutely still while she pulls and shrugs herself into a leather and rubber jacket with buckles and straps and zips, and a single fingerless mitt for the left hand.

'Why leather?' I ask, gripped with curiosity, wanting a beginner's feel for the basics.

'I chose leather.'

We came in by the back door, next to the creek, because out the front is the range. Attached to the clubhouse, like a long patio, there's a slab of concrete with fifteen shooting bays, each one separated by a low wooden screen. Fifty metres away over neatly mown grass, the target stalls look like a double row of flat hutches, and behind these there's a free-standing brick wall. That's in case anyone misses. On the left of the range is the creek; on the right, a creosoted picket fence, waist high. People walk by, but apparently that's OK. Before anyone starts shooting, a red flag will be raised on top of the back wall, and another one on the roof of the clubhouse.

'Er . . .' I don't know quite how to put this to Maria. 'Where's everyone else?'

'Jack and John will be along in a minute.'

'Just the three of you?'

'We're the regulars. And Ken the secretary's gone on holiday.'

Ken Willis had been my first point of contact at the club; he was helpful and encouraging and assured me that new members were always welcome, even though I hadn't shot a .22 rifle since I was twelve.

'We'll take anyone.'

'I'm from England.'

'Even so.'

At the Sydney Olympics, at about four in the morning, an Australian world champion lost the gold medal in double-trap shooting to a farmer's son from Hampshire. This was celebrated in Britain as a major upset, a significant chip at the Cringe, as if every Australian sport must by definition be in a better state than ours. But Manly Bowls Club had resorted to Bruce Malouf, and the Rifle Club was fighting for survival.

'More time and space for me to get in some practice, then,' I say selfishly, happily, perhaps even rubbing my hands together.

'Right,' Maria says. 'Yes, mate. Only the thing is. You know what? You're not actually allowed to shoot with us.'

I knew there had to be a catch. There's a special public health restriction concerning English nationals and firearms during an Ashes series. The risk is simply too great. *After England's second batting collapse of the match an unnamed man repeatedly shot an effigy of Shane Warne, and then turned the gun on himself.*

'Unlicensed, you can't even *touch* a gun.' Maria clips her .22 to her jacket. 'Don't worry,' she adds, 'we'll sort something out. You wait and see.'

John and Jack have now arrived, wrapped up against the inside-cold of the afternoon. Jack Astley is seventy-two years old, fit, with a white buzz cut and green-blue eyes and steel-rimmed Reactolite specs. He's sitting on one of the benches and eating his pie, quilted lumberjack shirt open over another shirt. He's a little deaf from the percussions of fifty-eight years at the Manly Rifle Club, but otherwise he's sprightly and as wise as any man should be after spending six decades in mortal danger twice a week.

'If it wasn't for the last minute,' he says, placing a darkroom timer and ear muffs on the rangemaster's elevated table out on the patio, 'nothing would ever get done.'

John Innes is Jack's junior. He's seventy-one. In that time he's managed to grow an impressive pair of kindly eyebrows and a thoughtful moustache. There's a sense of capability about him, but also of sadness, the kind of man perfectly able to kill his own dinner but not entirely happy about doing so. John owns four handguns and six longarms, and most of them are in the back of his disorderly pickup truck. He shows them to me one by one. His air rifle has a stock so beautiful, the grain of the bleached wood so straight and wide, it should have been a cricket bat.

'Walnut's the best,' he says. 'It's stable and it looks really nice.'

John is nostalgic for better days, when every teenager had a rabbit rifle. Fifty years ago, in the War Against Rabbits, clusters of boys used to gather in Sydney's Central Station, guns over their shoulders, and take the train into the country.

'Things aren't quite so easy these days.'

Specifically since 1996, when a lone gunman went into the Broad Arrow Café in Port Arthur in Tasmania, and shot dead twenty people.

Even before that, competitive shooting had had a troubled history in Australia. One of the major complaints the officer-class settlers had in the early nineteenth century was the lack of sport. They didn't mean games, but 'game', live-target shooting. As late as 1865, a letter in the London sporting chronicle *Bell's Life* reveals the limited imagination of some of the sportsmen recently arrived from Britain. 'We need to create in the southern hemisphere an exact counterpart of that country which is so dear to most of us.' And then fill it with creatures we'll shoot.

Australia's indigenous game was no sport at all. In 1867, Prince Alfred shot dead fifty-two possums, but found the massacre so dreary he left most of them hanging in the trees. Then he killed 416 rabbits, before lunch, helping to explain why adventurous Australian sportsmen preferred the challenge of cricket. Rabbits, one of the plagues of Australia, were first brought in for sport. In the absence of 'proper game', the new gentry also imported the fox and the sparrow, but ultimately rugby league proved more compelling than murdering imported songbirds.

Jack hoists the two red flags and shuts the back door. I'm not allowed to shoot, so I watch Maria and John. They have thirty minutes, timed by the clock on Jack's desk. They lie in the prone position and each aims at five black targets on a white ground, in the shape of a five on a dice. To aid concentration, silence is observed, apart from regular and abrupt loud bangs. Those are exactly the kind of noises that could put a person off. As could the evocative smell from spent brass cartridge cases, like sparklers, or the sight of a couple of mums with pushchairs strolling along the far side of the fence. Some kids on bikes pass them in the opposite direction.

While John and Maria compare results, Jack and I take some chairs out the back to warm up in the sun.

'The biggest time was after the war,' Jack tells me. 'We had a Spitfire pilot.'

Jack is modest, charming, and the Firearms Licensing Department of the Sydney Police has saved me the embarrassment of attempting to compete against him.

'I did shoot for Australia a bit,' he eventually admits,

and in 1961 he was the inaugural Australian National Small Bore Champion. He won a badge, a sash and a rifle, but missed the presentation because he had to drive back down from Brisbane for a normal Monday's work in the post office.

He still consistently gets the highest scores in the club, but his joints can seize up and when he shoots from the prone position Maria and John sometimes have to get on either side of him and haul him back to his feet. He smiles, but I don't think he finds it funny.

'Shooting's a young person's game.' Jack sighs. 'After twenty-nine, the eyesight goes. Then you're struggling.'

'Ever think of trying bowls?'

'Nah,' Jack chuckles. 'I'm not old enough yet for bowls. I'm only seventy-two. All we want is they let us carry on shooting.'

'They' is the government, because by law a new member now has a twenty-eight-day cooling-off period, a three-month trial, and a series of written and practical tests before being allowed to join a friendly bunch of people in an agreeable activity somewhere like the Manly Small Bore Rifle Club. The whole process can take six months to a year. Compare that to netball. Buy some pumps. Off you go. Or the camera club, where Jack increasingly spends his time, aiming, shooting, entering competitions.

As we're chatting, a police car scrunches over the gravel of the track. It pulls up in front of us and I fear the worst. The non-driving policeman, shades on, elbow out the window, tells us they've had a complaint. That's it: some-one phoned in and mentioned that every Wednesday and Saturday people shoot guns where children like to ride their bikes. But it's not that. Some kids have been reported for hitting golf balls into the creek. Have we seen anything? Even the crime is connected to sport, so we don't dob them in. The police car moves off.

Maria then comes out waving her phone, and she's furious. She's just been told by the Firearms Registry that if I'm going to shoot we have to go to the Sydney International Shooting Centre. This is the latest diversion in an absurd bureaucratic runaround. First of all, Maria asked permission for me to shoot at Manly with the rifle fixed to a bench and chained securely in place. No. With the rifle fixed to a bench, chained down, and under the close supervision of three adult permit-holding club members. Um. No.

The latest news is that I can shoot at the International Centre if I take my passport and pay fifty dollars.

'That sounds easy.'

'Too easy. It says you can do this in the brochures, but every shooter in Sydney knows that shooting by visitors is suspended.'

Also, I'm supposed to arrange my visit to the International Shooting Centre through a registered travel agent. The Firearms Registry do not have a list of registered travel agents. Nor do they have an e-mail address for the International Shooting Centre.

'I'm going to go down there,' Maria says. 'I'm going to take my rifle.'

'No, no,' I say, 'it's not worth it, Maria, calm down,' but then I see what she means. She's going to take her rifle so that I can shoot it. 'Oh. Thanks, thanks Maria. That would be great.'

Maria Silva is adamant that I, or anyone else with an interest, should be able in Australia to shoot a rifle for sport. She's an unquenchable enthusiast for her club and the sport of shooting in general, which is hardly surprising. You'd have to be mustard keen, considering the difficulties, or you wouldn't go anywhere near it.

I remember why I'm here, to beat the Australians, but in no time at all we seem to have ended up on the same team. It's Maria and me, Jack and John, the four of us on the road against the might of the Australian government, and headed for the Sydney International Shooting Centre. On the way there in his practical man's pickup, John Innes tells me everything I need to know about shooting, and perhaps a little more than that. In fact, the last time my head contained so much information about firearms was after reading a Tom Clancy novel, and one of those was enough.

The average age of shooters in New South Wales is forty-seven, and registered numbers are dwindling. Despite the government's safety concerns and other obstacles to getting a permit, the shooters don't die from accidents or rampages, but from old age, or the frustration of trying to keep their clubs alive. Shooting in Australia might already be dead, if it wasn't for the Olympics.

Australia buys into the Olympic ideal, embracing the modern calculation that success in Olympic sport equals the superiority of a way of life (it doesn't, of course, it suggests superiority at sport). Australia also buys into the ideal that customers in coffee shops ought not to have their heads blown apart by a gun nut with a 5.56 mm semi-automatic rifle. This means that target shooting needs to achieve the difficult trick of producing Olympic medallists without official encouragement.

The medals on offer mean the sport is unlikely ever to be abandoned, especially as Australian shooting has a distinguished Olympic history. As far back as 1900, in Paris, Donald Mackintosh won gold and bronze in two Olympic shooting competitions involving live pigeons. These days, they control their pigeons in Paris with poisoned bread. It's quieter, and requires no Australians.

Olympic success, more than the Ashes or any other contest with England, remains the measure of Australia's sporting achievement. This is because Olympic failure was also its primary catalyst. Or at least, a potent combination of failure and English snickering. At the Montreal Olympics in 1976 Australia won a dribble of medals, four of them bronze, and only one silver, in men's hockey. This was not the high-vitamin Australia we recognise today, or even the triumphant rise-and-shine swimming and tennis-playing Australia of the 1950s and '60s. The British press couldn't help it. If they'd kept quiet, Australia might sensibly have accepted a limited sporting future alongside other nations with a similar population, like Sri Lanka, or Yemen. Instead, the *Guardian* had to go and say that Australia was like a 'middle-aged athlete gone flabby', and no middle-aged athlete need take that on the chin. By the time of the Sydney Olympics in 2000, Australia was winning a torrent of fifty-eight medals, sixteen of them gold.

The Sydney International Shooting Centre, usually called Cecil Park because it's shorter, is a remnant of those Olympics, one of several state-of-the-art facilities purpose-built for the Sydney games. It is a simple structure, a stand-alone barn of galvanised steel and concrete, looking solid and stubborn in a vast area of cleared bushland to the west of the city. It is also very cold, and nearly completely empty. Concrete hallways chill and echo, unused plastic chairs tip forward onto empty plastic tables, and furled parasols don't quite hide the faded logo for *Sydney 2000*. In just one area, for the .22 rifles, there are sixty shooting bays. Today, a Saturday, there are four shooters.

This, I suppose, is what happens afterwards. This is part of the legacy that Olympic hosts like to tout. The British, for example, have already identified shooting for London 2012 as a 'major Olympic sport, and in the top six in terms of the number of medals available'. That's Peter Keen, a consultant for UK Sport, who adds, without much respect; 'I don't want to disrespect our shooters, but . . . if we could learn to shoot straight, there are a heck of a lot of medals out there.'

But what happens afterwards? In the air-rifle hall are another sixty bays and two girls in their mid-teens from the Australia youth team. I have a brief fantasy recruiting them as deadly female teenage assassins. It's steady work, and not just every four years. We'll tour European capitals, and when not on duty in black catsuits the girls will accompany me in ball gowns to glam elitist casinos.

I have to be the chief (in a dinner jacket) because the government refuses to budge on a foreigner firing a one-shot .22 rifle, even in the nation's premier shooting centre, under supervision (Maria repeats the previous offer involving benches and chains and responsible adults). However, I *am* allowed to shoot a multi-fire pistol, of the type easily concealed in a sports bag on my way to the Commonwealth Bank of Australia.

Instead of stopping to search for the logic of this decision, I follow John Innes to the pistol range. An Asian and a one-armed Paralympian are out-cooling each other at fifty metres, but I ignore them as John gives me his Unique .22 Rimfire, a handgun made in the Basque country, with five rounds in the magazine. This is an

Olympic event called standard pistol, and I ask John what I need to be a good pistol shooter.

'Short arms,' he says.

I have arm-length arms, and I'm holding a handgun, shakily, and for once I'm not that bothered about finding my killer instinct. Not just at the moment. I'm a cop, I'm a robber, an Olympic contender. This is the imaginative terrain.

Finally, I'm about to compete in Australia.

Blam! A victory! We beat the Australian government. *Blam! Blam! Blam!* A defeat! Only two shots on target. *Blam!* Hit! A revelation! I now know for certain that Orwell was talking nonsense.

* * *

Serious sport has nothing to do with fair play. It is bound up with hatred, jealousy, boastfulness, disregard of all rules and sadistic pleasure in witnessing violence: in other words it is war minus the shooting.

George Orwell, 'The Sporting Spirit'

This is the boat used to float a thousand arguments opposed to sport and the shadow it sometimes casts. From George Orwell, of all people, who's usually so reliable. The extract comes from a column Orwell wrote for *Tribune* in a series called 'I Write As I Please', and the first time 'The Sporting Spirit' was published in book form, it came with an editor's apology. The editor explains that this and similar squibs need to be read in their proper context, as drudge columns for a polemical newspaper: 'Written under these conditions they cannot be considered in the same category as the other essays.'

In other words, Orwell as columnist needs to be treated with caution, a warning that goes missing in later editions of his collected prose. In the final sentence of 'The Sporting Spirit', Orwell decides 'there are quite enough real causes of trouble already, and we need not add to them by encouraging young men to kick each other on the shins amid the roars of infuriated spectators'.

But sport doesn't add to the trouble, it replaces it. Certainly something like this is going on in the conflation of two of the great foundation myths of modern Australia: on the one hand the First World War catastrophe at Gallipoli; on the other, Australian trial and effort on the playing fields of the twentieth century.

Despite today's perception of Australians as winners, the national-military myth of Gallipoli is a story of loss. Or so it seems at first sight. The United States had to fight a war of independence to forge a nation free of British influence. The Australians took a less matter-of-fact approach, and Gallipoli represents the nation-building civil war Australia successfully avoided. It remains a potent symbol not because Australians were defeated by Turks, but because the digger spirit was never conquered despite an incompetent British chain of command.

This is General Sir John Monash, corps commander of the Australian forces on the Western Front, praising Anzac soldiers at Gallipoli: 'Our boys, capably led, can give the British regulars points and a beating at any part of the game, whether it be digging a trench, or in a bayonet assault, or in steadiness under fire, or in boiling the billy or in ambulance work, or in even cheerfully suffering fatigue and privations, or in marching, or personal bravery.' Which leaves the British with sewing, the only military accomplishment Monash fails to mention. In this way, a defeat is turned into a victory, and the military shambles in the Dardanelles is worth the Australian sacrifice.

Steve Waugh took his cricket team to visit Gallipoli before the Ashes tour of England in 2001, making a direct connection between Australian sport and the freedom-fighting Anzac tradition. PE is obligatory in schools, and in New South Wales so is the teaching of the Gallipoli campaign in classes seven to ten. The values of the Anzac soldiers, the diggers, are thought to be representative of a distinctly Australian way of life, and they include stoicism, physical toughness, positivity and plain speak-ing, the same qualities ideally revealed and admired in Australian sportspeople. It was therefore no surprise when Ricky Ponting's 2005 Ashes squad followed Waugh's precedent. Before landing in England, they stopped off in France and paid their respects at the Australian Memorial Park at Fromelles, near the infamous Aubers Ridge. Fifty-three thousand Australians died on the Western Front, four times the number lost in Turkey.

The Ashes are serious sport, but they're not war, barely even a faint echo of war, a hint of a shadow of a reminder. Mike Marqusee, the sharp American writer on cricket, memorably wrote that Orwell's 'equation trivialises both activities'. In helping to define relations between Britain and Australia, as it did in the twentieth century, sport has been a substitute for war, a refinement, an improvement.

Blam! This is my revelation: if sport is war without the shooting, what is the sport of shooting? War without the shooting, with shooting. But that doesn't make it war.

To fully appreciate this, best to move away from the white Olympic elephant at Cecil Park, and shuffle humbly back to sport in and for the community. Maria is determined that I shouldn't go away disappointed. I *will* shoot a rifle, among Australians. In the meantime, she's driven me round most of Sydney, introduced me to the shooting community, and shared her limitless enthusiasm.

'You should move here. Yeah, mate. Get a job. Bring the family. You can start out at my place.'

Everything I believe in, everything positive sport can do to people and for people, starts here with a shared interest and the unconditionally warm welcome offered by anyone like Maria. She wants me to see club shooting at its best. She therefore takes me to a restaurant, at Sydney's Austrian Club.

'This is where we shoot air rifles,' she says, but there's no obvious range. 'Right here.' And she gestures a little impatiently at the restaurant tables, and the signs over the kitchen hatch saying 'Hofküche' and 'Stammtisch', 'Schnitzels' and 'Schnapps'. Perhaps they humanely cull any customer with a lisp. The Austrian and Australian flags hang either side of the club's eagle insignia, and on the door to the toilets there's an Alp poster saying 'Austria, Europe with a Difference'. It might as well say 'Australia – Europe with a Difference'. Australia can comfortably, even obviously, contain Austria.

'Where do you actually shoot these air rifles?' I ask, still confused, 'and when?'

'After the customers have left. Then we get cracking.'

At the far end of the restaurant is a panelled wall with inoffensive paintings of still-life fruit and landscapes. When the restaurant is empty, each panel above waist height hinges upward like the flap of an ice-cream van, pictures still attached. Underneath, running the length of the far wall of the restaurant, is a row of nine targets. *Hande Hoch!* It's a shooting gallery. The club shoots air

44

rifles at ten metres over tables still laid up with red and white tablecloths, aiming over the heads of flowers in vases and glinting steel salt cellars.

Now ten metres may sound more than twice as easy as twenty-five metres, and five times as easy as the fifty metres they were shooting at Cecil Park, but shooters aren't a marginalised group for nothing. As the distance gets shorter, they make the targets smaller. These ones are a ridiculous five centimetres across, and the bull is so small it's not a circle but a half-millimetre dot.

It's also competitive. This Tuesday evening at the Austrian Club, the Sydney *Österreichischer Schützverein* is taking part in the Teutonia August Open Postal Shoot. Each person will take sixty shots at sixty separate targets, one target at a time. If you were to hit near-perfect bulls with every shot, you could stack up your sixty targets and see daylight through a hole in the middle. That would be grand. Other air rifle clubs from all over Australia send in their cards and a winner is declared.

Most of the members of the Austrian Club are called John, perhaps for security reasons, and they teach me how to shoot. Or if I'd been allowed, and firearms licensing had been less restrictive and more logical, they would have done so. It's very important, if you do beat the government, any government, even the Australian government, not to brag about it. You could get into trouble. Also, it wouldn't be sporting.

So, by pure observation, I'd have to guess it's not about muscles but about bones. 'A muscle that twitches,' one of the Johns says, 'has tension in it.' The keen shooters splint the natural good work of their skeletons by wearing rigid rubber suits, and boots with stiff flat soles. They look ridiculous, and can't unbend their legs when they walk.

The hardened trousers therefore have zips up the back to release the knees, when necessary, but these suits are just the beginning, the visibly ridiculous consequences of the pursuit of sporting excellence.

Try and be all bone, no muscle. In this sport, muscles are unreliable. Bones are the thing, and this explains why from a standing position women are better shots than men, because they can fit the bone of the elbow onto the bone of the hip, creating a rigid prop for the body of the rifle. This rests on the back of the hand, across the knuckles, with the fingers pointing back at the throat. Imagine the Egyptian walk but with the hand turned back as if threatening your own windpipe. It's not natural; it's a skill, and you have to learn how to do it.

Back at the Manly Rifle Club I'd asked Jack for some tips. Just in case I ever had a chance to shoot and seeing as I didn't really know what I was doing, except having a go.

'Ah,' Jack said, an ageless fount of wisdom. 'You don't need to know what you're doing to succeed.'

'Really? That's fantastic news.'

'But for continuing success,' he added, 'you need to know what you've done.'

Repeat the same set of movements again and again, like a monastic ritual, an access to well-being. Don't close one eye, because it makes you tense. Instead use a blind, a piece of card which sticks out to the left of the sight. This is the reason for those head-band contraptions that make Olympic shooters (and archers, too) look like they've recently survived a highly technical road accident. If you fire to the right, you've got a problem called the Trigger. Right elbow up a bit. The right hand, the trigger hand, should hardly grip at all.

Ready? A top shooter will shoot between heartbeats.

This requires a controlled, meditational awareness of your own body. Inhale half a breath, small exhale, hold it, shoot. Bingo. Hit the bull which is a half-millimetre dot. Ten points. Repeat sixty times, win.

But after forty shots I'd have been exhausted, if the government had allowed me to shoot. My vision would have started to blur and my arms to ache and my breathing would have grown ragged. That is, if I'd also resisted the urge to snatch up a gun and wheel round and embark on a hip-held single-shot air-gun rampage, though there's no evidence the Firearms Registry has ever saved anyone, and I didn't do that, and never would have. So with a gun in my hands what *would* I have done?

I'd have scored about 200 out of a possible 400 in forty shots, and then I'd have needed a serious sit-down.

Sitting down, my eye is caught by a display of plates high up on one of the walls. Hand-painted on each plate is the name of that year's club champion, the *Schützenkönig*. Or in the case of Maria, the *Schützenkönigin*. I watch her shoot fast and accurately, hitting the bull about seven times out of ten, and it's absurd to think I could ever have beaten the number-eleven-ranked woman at air rifle in all Australia.

As a spectator sport shooting has its limits, unless you're a springer spaniel. But actually doing it is compelling, and it's a shame that it's an increasingly difficult sport to pursue. As Jack told me, explaining why he went to the national championships for twenty-five years in succession, he loved the camaraderie, the standard of conduct, the sense of responsibility. Shooting encourages the same virtues claimed for any sport.

It's true we don't *need* shooting. Sport is unnecessary. We don't need football, or cricket, or paragliding. If shooting *were* necessary, we'd be in a sorry state. It's a sport that teaches concentration and the bothersome connection between hard work and success. A good shooter will also cultivate a kind of relaxed rigour, a disciplined serenity. Demonised by the anti-gun lobby, marginalised by mainstream sports, these sharpshooters are the most responsible, calm people on earth. It doesn't pay to get uptight, not with so many guns around.

At the end of the evening, we vacuum the flattened pellets from the carpet beneath the panelled wall, which is now back in place, the pictures of Alps and flowers looking bland and whistling innocently. We gather round one of the long tables and drink Gösser beer and schnapps, telling shooting stories, cursing the government. Shooters are quite normal and enjoyable company, I think. Later on, John Innes gets out the photos of his holiday, shooting machine guns and anti-tank rifles somewhere outdoors in Wyoming.

I did eventually get to play and beat an Australian at bowls.

Frank Geer is back in his office at North Manly Bowls Club. He's not full-time and he's not paid, but he cheerily tells me he's here most of the time, and he's working. His wife is feeling much better, yes thank you, and we can have that bowls lesson now.

As well as exercise and an outdoor tan, bowls offers the senior citizen a reason for keeping up appearances. It's hard to let yourself go when a condition of tournament bowls is spotless shoes. Frank is immaculate, his combed-back hair as white and gleaming as his shoes and trousers. Originally from Essex, he arrived in Australia in 1988, after a contract in Saudi Arabia.

'I went back home and I couldn't get warm. Never. Not once. Brrr. Then I came out here.'

'So now you're an Australian bowler?'

'I'm still from Essex. They love their sport out here, and I support their teams. In everything except the cricket.'

Ah, I think, Frank's soul remains intact. I clap my hands together and eye the set of round black bowls Frank has brought out for me. Or not quite round. 'Let's get started.'

'Safety first,' Franks says.

In bowls, safety involves not falling over. After a certain age, this is most important. The two main hazards are the low wall around the perimeter of the green (Frank steps over forwards and does a comical trip to make his point), and then the bowls themselves. (Frank mimes standing on a bowl. 'You're gawn!' he says. 'Break your legs, back, anything!') I'm surprised the government hasn't banned it, and wonder whether to take out insurance. Frank doesn't laugh. New bowlers have to sign an indemnity form before playing. Frank then gives them a certificate to say they've been through his safety briefing.

'Oh. And always roll bowls with the soles of your feet.'

'Is that safer?'

'No. That's to keep your shoes clean.'

Frank shows me the basics. Roll the bowl smooth and sweet and low from the middle finger of the hand. He is patient yet insistent, a good teacher, but I sense that even in bowls it's possible to overcoach, analysing posture, delivery, follow-through, breathing. If it wasn't for coaching, most sports might have been mastered by now.

The close-cropped rink is a sunlit and peaceful Eden as I get to grips with old man's marbles, one of the great Empire sports. W.G. Grace turned to bowls once he'd finished playing cricket, and in 1903 was the first president of the English Bowls Association. The Australian lawn bowlers had toured in 1901, so he could be sure of a decent contest, though already it was difficult to know whether they treasured our games because they loved or hated us. In the nineteenth century, the USA invented gridiron, basketball, baseball and volleyball. This was the more obvious rejection, devising entirely new sports. Australia had Australian Rules, but otherwise set about beating us at the games we thought we knew best. These games then became a large part of what we now have in common, along with the Queen, like the moon above us, distant but dimly reassuring.

Sport and royalty might even have provided a formula for eternal light, if only the Australians hadn't insisted on winning all the time. I therefore challenge Frank to a game. I get thrashed, and this isn't a sport where gritting your teeth and getting stuck in is going to help. On the green next to us, the club's oldest active member is trundling down the bowls at eighty-six years old. When he gets to the other end, his wife helps him pick them up again with a patented steel bowl-picker-upper. She is eighty-three and a half.

'Can I play against them?'

'Look,' Frank says. 'If you're really that keen, you can play against my wife.'

Fay is Australian, and the last time I was here she was in hospital. But this is no time for sentiment. I remember Mr Newton and stiffen my temperament, harden my attitude. I go through Frank's checklist and bowl smooth and sweet and low, spiking my tactics with forethought and malice. I may be about to beat Australian Fay Geer at lawn bowls. It's a tense moment, even though Fay was in hospital because she's had a stroke. Her bowling arm is paralysed, so she's learning again with her left hand. She's finding it difficult to get the correct weight, and is regularly bowling too fast and too far. Also, she's full of the joy of being alive and out of hospital, laughing, joking, and not much caring who wins.

In fact, when it comes to caring too much, on North Manly bowling green it's me who's grumbling and chuntering because the trouble with bowls is that you always think you're about to get it together. You can play a truly awful shot, in the context of the match, and still be only a couple of metres out. It's a distance I feel I could rectify, that same afternoon, but I can't. I twice put the bias on the wrong side so the bowl ends up halfway to Melbourne.

On the deciding bowl, Fay gives it too much and it smashes into the ditch. I win. At the first time of asking, I've beaten an Australian fast bowler.

'Never mind,' Fay says. 'Let's have some tea and cake. Are you married at the moment?'

Later, as I'm coming out of the clubhouse, glowing with victory and tea and cake and a good laugh with Fay and Frank, Gerry Muoio is waiting. He steps out of the shadow of the overhanging roof.

'So how about we play some *bocce*?'

'Gerry, would you say you're a competitive person?'

'You gotta be a good loser.'

'Ah.'

'And a bad loser.'

'Oh.'

'Shit yeah.'

'Go on then. Let's have a game of *bocce*.'

Gerry gleefully unzips his *bocce* bag, which is nearby, open and ready by the side of the rink, in fact. He tells me that when he first arrived in Australia they were always trying to get him to bowl.

'I say no. I wanna roll a *bocce*. I have a try with a bowl. I a like it. I'm a gonna stick into it.'

Then he tells me why both bowling and *bocce* are good for the soul. 'You forget everything what's in the family. Relax. We have a nicer cuppa tea or a few drinks with the mates.'

And then we have a roll with the *bocce*. Of all the many analogies sport so teasingly throws up, this is my new favourite. *Bocce*, which are heavy round balls, a little bigger than a bowl, go dead straight. Unlike British and Australian lawn bowls, they are perfectly spherical and rational and have no bias. It should be easy, but it's harder than bowls, much trickier to get in close to the jack. Those old pre-industrial bowls get closer to the target by starting with a noticeable bias.

Gerry thrashes me out of sight.

'Any time of a day,' he says. 'Have a roll. Shit yeah.'

Shooting and bowls vindicate sport as a lifetime activity, a lifelong experience. Games aren't something to put by and lose in a closet, the discarded bats and balls neglected with the imprisoned and whimpering inner child. In many years to come, even half as indomitable as Fay Geer, I hope me and my inner child will be bright and breezy and out there like Gerry and Frank, like Jack and John, playing some vital game or other and taking on the world.

Frank comes out to see me off, cup and saucer in his hands. 'Good start,' he says, 'but next time we'll see how you go under pressure. Looking forward to the cricket?'

'Probably,' I say.

Second Test

I thought stuff that stiff-upper-lip crap. Let's see how stiff it is when it's split.

Jeff Thomson, *Thommo*, 1980

The trouble with Australia is that it's nearly all outside. You can't avoid the outdoors, and that's where most Australians spend their days. By coming in their winter, I'd hoped to cancel out the accepted Australian advantage of the weather, and I was even looking forward to some rain, as an occasional excuse to stay inside and read a book. It's an established phenomenon that *Rain Saves England* and, ever hopeful, I was all set to note down the changing winter weather on a daily basis. I gave up.

Unless I suggest otherwise, assume the sky is vast and blue and the day hot and bright. Green parrots swoop in pairs between buildings and trees. Whatever clouds there are, in the very early morning, look like the other side of ours. We have the grey belly, they have the dazzling cotton wool of the sunny side up, the version usually seen from planes.

The weather, though, isn't the whole story. Admittedly,

it does nothing to get in the way of Australians being better at sport than us, but in other countries with the same humid subtropical climate as Sydney the sun sends potential Olympians scurrying in search of shade. This means that much of Indonesia and the western coast of Turkey are as short of number three batsmen as they are of skin cancer clinics. The long hot summer and mild winter aren't reasons enough in themselves; they need added input from an outsider sensibility.

Europeans arrived in Australia with a displaced northern belief that sunshine must be good for you. In a temperate climate the sun is growth and life. Get out in it, hunt, forage and sport in it before the cold comes back, and the rain, and repeated documentaries about Torvill and Dean on BBC2. The Australians get out in it, and they stay out, as if December in Grimsby was always a couple of months away. The sun then shines and shines, and before anyone realises what's happening, there's a nation of world-champion log-choppers in the Australian green and gold.

This is how the Australian winter works on a northerner like me. The sun is always shining, and I want to be out in it. There are playing fields round every corner and the beach is two minutes away on foot even if I amble very slowly, in flip-flops. Why would I not go out?

I wake up, the sun is hat on and hip-hip-hooraying, and I'm off in search of Manly sunshine sports. What am I going to beat the Australians at *next*? The golf course is a short walk away, past the Boy Charlton Swim Centre with its Olympic pool, and some tennis courts where a plastic tarpaulin announces 'Open 7 Days a Week, Day and Night'. At the Rec by the Swindon Old Town Gardens we had one tarmac tennis court. It was never open, but someone had a key. No one knew who that someone was. This is why I nod sympathetically when tennis fans moan about Wimbledon and points being settled by one or two shots maximum per rally. For me, tennis has always been that way, except I also have to fetch the balls.

I therefore keep walking past the 24/7 tennis courts and the universal Manly background of kids having ball-playing fun on open green fields. I have a membership appointment with the captain and vice-president of the Manly Golf Club, founded 1903, and sufficiently established by 1909 for the *Sydney Morning Herald* to report that the 'course may be said to be one for good golfers where good shots meet with their reward. Heavy trouble awaits the man who makes a mistake.'

This is why I'm wearing a suit. Don't want to make any mistakes. When I get there, acting as adult as I can, I pretend to notice that the clubhouse is an effective mix of several architectural styles. The elegant white sweep of the Mediterranean is made imposing by the addition of Georgian columns. The clubhouse at Manly Golf Club is Australian-classic, from 1924, and it's an eloquent reminder to anyone who may have forgotten that Manly is an elite Group One Australian golf course.

Denise, the friendly English secretary, shows me upstairs to wait in the restaurant. 'Ken and Bob are still out on the course,' she says. 'Can I get you a drink?'

My small lager comes in a quaint dimpled glass with a handle, reminding me of English pubs from when I was underage. The inside of the clubhouse has something familiar about it, and now I realise why. It's like a special treat to an adult place with parents; I know it's supposed to be fun but I feel awkward and wish I was somewhere else. There are plush carpets, expensive chairs, and wooden honours boards on the walls. It's an unforgivable trick, an outing to the entrance hall of a private prep school to meet the headmaster. That would explain my sense of dread.

I don't dare look too closely into any of the side rooms, because in golf clubs I never feel far from disapproval. In golf, it saves time to assume you're always doing something wrong – standing in someone's peripheral vision, stepping on the line of a putt, your shadow's in the way, you're playing out of turn, you just said fuck in front of the captain. There are any number of small ways of doing something *appalling*, and you won't know what they are until you hear an insistent tutting sound and receive a letter in the next day's post from the Etiquette Committee.

At least, that's how it is in England. Giving everyone a fair go is not golf's guiding principle. In private golf clubs, a prospective member has to overcome all sorts of financial and social obstacles. He may then join the waiting list. Manly is a private golf club, but I'm hoping to become a temporary member for as long as it takes to beat the locals. This is only going to happen if golf in Australia has escaped its fate in the traditional clubs of England, as a self-satisfied agent of social segregation. Community sport at its best is a force for good, and a breaker of social boundaries. Golf, however, is fenced-off, forbidding, divisive.

In his book *Empire Games*, Roger Hutchinson describes 'the unique and seminal creation of the British bourgeois intelligence: the club'. What he doesn't say is that the bourgeois intelligence can be good, and it can be bad. And the worst aspects of the bourgeois intelligence are enshrined in a particular kind of golf club.

This is why intelligent people who like the game over-state their case, like the novelist Tim O'Grady, boosting golf as 'a non-violent sport in which civility and generosity are paramount and dishonesty is a disgrace'. If that's true, then why are there so many rules? Because otherwise golfers would cheat. The code of sportsmanship and decency has to be constantly reinforced by rules and penalties because it doesn't flow naturally from the game itself. Golfers are even advised to carry a rule book with them in their bags. In a similar way, the sham familiarity of 'Jack' and 'Tiger' smudges the truth that golf isn't very friendly. Everyone gets their own ball, because no one wants to share.

Admittedly, the changing rooms are clean and there are towels in the bathrooms. This confirms my suspicion that golf is sport for people who don't like sport. Or an extension of the same idea – sport for people who don't like people. It's possible to play golf perfectly happily alone. If, that is, the rest of the members allow it.

I meet Bob the captain and Ken the vice-president in the downstairs bar. I am uptight and despite the stiffness of my suit in a dreadful state for small-bore shooting or toadying, while Bob and Ken have just come off the course wind-blown and red-faced, two men in early retirement, I think, who are refusing to unlearn the habit of activity. I accept another small lager in a dimpled glass with a handle. We all take a seat, like a job interview, Bob and Ken on one side of the table and me on the other.

'Temporary membership,' I remind them, as politely as I can. 'English, visitor, sports book, fantastic club, *fantastic* club, shapely old course. *Love* the game of golf.'

Bob and Ken listen and tut and grimace and chew their lips and shake their heads. It is, indeed, tough for them to let me on the Manly golf course. My short-term membership proposal will have to be approved by the board, and I understand this. This small, or not so small, acreage of Manly represents a conquered territory, tranquil and controlled, paid for. Of course théy should want to check up on me. It makes sense to be wary of the barbarians at the gate.

Then they ask how good a player I am, as if that makes a difference, and because it might make a difference, I lie. These are Australians, remember, and they immediately sense a point of vulnerability, a weakness. This is either true, or the Cringe has me believe it, but in any case Bob and Ken hear my claims to a respectable handicap and strike without hesitation. They immediately seize the opportunity to put me under pressure.

'How about a trial hit with the president?'

I bluff it out, a new confident England in the style of the twenty-first century. 'Sure. As soon as you like.'

'Let's say tomorrow then. Two o'clock.'

One of golf's quaint boasts is that the handicap system makes it a competitive game for players of varying ability. If you're a member of a club, every meaningful round is taken into account, good as well as bad, and somewhere between these two impostors every golfer finds a level. My absolute best ever performance is eighteen shots over par, but I haven't played for a couple of years so it's essential that when asked for my handicap, I don't say eighteen.

I said eighteen.

Eighteen! The course record is held by Jack Nicklaus, who shot a sixty-two. This means I'm saying I'll get within twenty-eight shots of Jack Nicklaus in 1971. Absurd!

This impetuous act of bravado cancels out the advantage I was intending to steal by exaggerating my handicap. It's not an auspicious start, especially when golf, I feel, is a sport where Australians are vulnerable. They have one player in the top twenty in the world, which is hard to explain as theirs is a sunny country with fine athletes and many pampered golf courses. There's also the brittle history of Greg Norman. Golf may be the only known sport in which Australians are famous for choking.

At the 1996 US Masters, Greg Norman set out on his final round at Augusta with a six-shot lead over Nick Faldo. This is the kind of lead that only a bunch of hardened incompetents, say the 1990s England cricket team, could squander. Greg was sensational. He fell apart, a study in sporting catastrophe, bogeying the ninth, tenth, eleventh, hitting the water at twelve, and then, just in case anyone thought he was getting it back together, in the water again at sixteen. The wheels came off, in spectacular fashion, and not just the wheels.

Meanwhile, the Englishman Nick Faldo gritted his teeth like an Australian, and hustled through to win.

I could go on. So I will. The Australian golfer Rod Pampling is the only man to lead the Open after the first round, and then miss the cut, at Carnoustie in 1999. In another reassuring memory, I was at St Andrew's for the Open in 1995. It was the first major golf tournament I'd watched live, and in real life I found the width of the first fairway at St Andrew's shocking. It's *easy*. Even I could have hit it, because it stretches most of the way to Edinburgh. Ian Baker-Finch, an Australian and winner of the Open four years earlier, stepped up to the tee. He missed the fairway. To the left, and by a mile. It was such an atrocious shot it must have taken stupendous natural ability simply to achieve the physics. Baker-Finch had been eaten and beaten by nerves, and he was living proof of the psychological seriousness of sport. It had unhinged him. With no tournament win after 1993, he retired and became a respected designer of other people's golf courses. With fairways providing generous margins of error to the left.

The next day, at two o'clock, I'm standing on the first tee at Manly Golf Club, in my hired shoes with my hired three wood in my hand, and the fairway is narrow on both sides. I tell myself I don't care. Just enjoy it. And because I'm good at self-deception, this is a strategy that almost works. I look appraisingly at the bunkers either side of the fairway, and the trees to the side of the bunkers. The first hole of Manly Golf Course, as apparently all golf holes do, is asking of me a question on the tee. And that question is: 'Am I correctly dressed?'

I have on my best trousers, cream-coloured, which I was saving for a special occasion, like a wedding. These trousers are visibly cheaper than those worn by Ken Munro and Gerry Elkan, respectively vice-president and president of Manly Golf Club. I have a blue polo shirt, but without recognisable logo, and I feel underdressed for golf's famously relentless examination of the individual. Except more naked than that, stripped of the security blanket that comes like a gift with team sports. I miss the reassurance of trust in others, and the licence to develop a deadly seriousness on someone else's behalf. I miss Maria and Jack and John.

Addressing my ball, in a team of one, I can't quite take it seriously enough. This is good. It means I relax. I swing through the ball which makes it off the ground, as high as many early biplanes. One of its engines then fails and it careens off right into a paperbark tree. But I'm away. At the second hole it takes me a mere two shots to reach the bottom of the creek in front of the green.

After that, I calm down a bit, and only lose one ball while discovering that in golf my relative youth counts for something. Not for intimidating Ken and Gerry, as I'd hoped, but being reasonably fit I can fire my ball in unlikely directions, run after it, and still arrive at the green at about the same time as they do. In this way, I also get to see more of the details of the landscaping, the astonishing papery bark on the paperbark trees, the herons and pelicans on the lagoon, the roots of eucalypts and grevilleas, occasionally coming across balls lost on earlier doomed expeditions, like the remains of former golfers.

Gerry Elkan is loose-limbed and tall, a former fast bowler of the type, I imagine, to think out a batsman. Though also, I decide after watching him miss a putt, the type to get intensely annoyed with any opening batsman not intelligent enough to get himself out-thought. Ken is shorter, pugnacious and energetic, looking about thirty years younger than he is, like someone who makes money in the morning, loses half of it in the afternoon, but can still put his feet up in the evening and laugh over a glass of wine. None of this had been immediately apparent to me during yesterday's interview in the clubhouse, but whatever its other shortcomings, golf like most sports does allow one human being a better idea of another.

My score is eighteen over after eleven holes, and I'm chuffed to bits because then the sun goes down and we have to stop, my impersonation of an eighteen-handicapper still vaguely intact. Or if not, Gerry is too courteous to say so. He went out of his way, near the tenth tee, to show me three yellow-faced cockatoos in a bush. He pointed out other birds as we went round, and named them, and explained that the most effective natural defence in Australia was inedibility. Gerry and Ken played their golf (briskly, because of recent trouble with slow play) like most people wander round their gardens, with a distracted air of ownership, routinely clearing water channels with the toe of a golf shoe and checking the placement of various bits and pieces. They tightened up ropes around 'Buggies This Way', and re-stuck the tin-plate signs for 'Ground Under Repair'.

Near the eleventh tee, Ken had peered into a flower bed at a plant he didn't recognise. 'That's not a native,' he said. 'I reckon one of the women must have put it in. It's a geranium or something.'

Golf has a greed for territory, reshaping natural landscape with a northern European idea of space, of fun. The course itself is then the setting for a certain kind of sporting narrative, eighteen connected episodes creating the story of a round of golf. In Australia, though, the landscape was once expressed by other, older stories.

It may be that Australians choke at golf out of guilt.

Manly was given its name in 1788 when the colony's first governor, Captain Arthur Phillip, sailed out on a reconnaissance from Botany Bay.

The boats, in passing near a point of land in this harbour, were seen by a number of men, and twenty of them waded into the water unarmed, received what was offered them and examined the boats with a curiosity that gave me a much higher opinion of them than I had formed from the behaviour of those seen in Captain Cook's voyage. And their confidence and manly behaviour made me give the name of Manly Cove to this place.

This report comes from Governor Phillip's first dispatch home, after only four months of settlement, and it shows that manliness is often on the European mind. The unarmed natives (the Kay-e-my-gal people), broad chests bared, may have seemed manly like bare-chested and unarmed boxers, a sport whose first rules of conduct had been codified in London forty years earlier by Jack Broughton. There were only two rules. Hit above the waist. Don't hit a man when he's down.

Otherwise all manoeuvres were legitimate, and Phillip's first initiative was kidnap. He sent out two of his lieutenants, Johnston and Ball, to find an Aboriginal man and bring him back alive. They caught two, at Collins Cove in Manly, but one escaped. They tried again, and came back with Bennelong and Colebee. Phillip claimed he was just opening a dialogue, but the natives weren't idiots. They had a sense of what was coming, and accordingly in 1790 they stuck the new governor with a twelve-foot spear. He survived. And although Phillip nobly ordered no reprisals be taken, the smallpox was already at work.

Later, the British would consolidate their invasion by changing the coastal landscape. According to Manly Golf Club's official history, the course was originally 'a snake-infested, heavily-timbered swamp, marshes and bogs'. These were eradicated, along with coarse natural grasses and 'rank vegetation'. Sand was pumped in to raise the fairways, drains were sunk, hollows and slopes moulded on the greens, and trees and shrubs planted to complement the carpet of salt-tolerant Kikuyu grass, imported from colonial east Africa.

This transformation, one among many, was considered a distinct improvement, because the first Europeans to set eyes on Manly were less than impressed. The place was mostly bush, an 'almost valueless tract of brush land'.

In fact, it was the premier site of Aboriginal culture in south-east Australia. That's why the Kay-e-my-gal people were here in numbers wading out towards Phillip's boat. Manly was where the saltwater tribes liked to be. Described by the British as 'individually robust and of large stature', the Aboriginal people who lived here were numerous and powerful because they ate well and slept well, the cove teeming with shellfish and the sandstone rock formations offering excellent shelter.

Manly therefore became the site of contact between cultures, the place where Europeans first encountered Aboriginal women, kidnapped Aboriginal men, and witnessed the spearing of Phillip. What happened in Manly determined the history that followed – the oppression of Aborigines, the development of Sydney, the shaping of modern Australia.

This story is now retold in the landscape, especially on the coastal fringe. Aboriginal people once complicated this territory with songs, rituals, religion. Their songlines are invisible pathways, chanted as stories, that map natural features while embodying a conception of the sacred, of mythic time and ancestral origin. The land itself was and is at the heart of Aboriginal culture, with every hill, valley and waterhole having its function in a systematic but unwritten whole. The land is existence and the law that governs behaviour. It is time itself.

Or it's a golf course. Take your pick. Golf is landscape simplified. Here are the trees, here the clearings, here the tracks (Buggies This Way), here the lakes and streams. Here is landscape as an obstacle to be overcome, a challenge to be met and conquered in spiked two-tone shoes.

Ken and Gerry reward my half-decent round of golf, my pressed trousers and my revivalist English pluck by suggesting I play with the fags.

'Sorry?'

'Join the fags, Richard.'

So not so impressed after all. Because they're not joking, and because I'm exhausted by pretending to be good at golf, I think I might cry.

'The Friday afternoon golfers,' Ken explains. 'They play every Friday.'

'In the afternoon,' Gerry adds helpfully. 'How long were you thinking of staying?'

Of course I wasn't really going to cry. Reminding myself I'm tough and anti-Australian and ready for anything, I narrow my eyes. 'How long? As long as it takes, Gerry.'

Come Friday, the clock showing just after twelve, I walk into the downstairs clubhouse bar in the same clothes as for my round with Gerry and Ken. I'm glad I've made the effort. The FAGs is the most informal gathering of golfers at Manly Golf Club, yet FAGs president John Johns is sitting officially behind a long table sorting out who tees off with who. He has ledgers and records and a special system of Friday afternoon handicaps. He's keeping everybody in order, a wiry chuckling old gent in a maroon jumper who looks younger than he is, however old he is, and I think he's quite old. It's the tan, and the brightness of eye that comes from regular outdoor exercise and chums who rip the piss.

'Nice to meet you,' John says, giving me a big scrunched-eye smile and a hard dry handshake that comforts like a leather steering wheel. 'You're Richard and we've been expecting you. Ready to go?'

We'll be playing two against two, for money, and it's not immediately clear to me how FAGs golf, which is informal, differs from the golf on Wednesdays and Saturdays, which is competitive.

'Otherwise why get out of bed?' my partner Richard Clark says. 'If you don't care who wins, why bother scoring?'

Actually, I don't always bother scoring, not the bad holes, but the money reassures me that this time, unlike Fay at bowls, the Australians want to win. I'm drawn with Richard against ex-policeman Steve Moran and John Mater. I check they have use of all their limbs. Steve's a big man and must have taken retirement early because he looks young enough to be bunking off. John, although older, *is* bunking off because he has the most thankless job in Sydney. He sells heaters. No wonder he can skip work on another glorious afternoon with more of the same forecast for the weekend. In this way, not selling heaters keeps a man in his sixties fit and cheery, but possibly also it lingers in the mind as a distraction to the total focus required of a winner. If he looks like getting ahead, I can ask him how's business.

Another promising sign is that the Manly Golf Club has a certain age profile. This means that unlike most Australian sportsmen, the golfers aren't backing themselves, not wholeheartedly. On the fourth, sixth, seventh, eighth, sixteenth and seventeenth holes there are emergency alarms connected directly to the hospital. This is in case anyone collapses. The red button is for dead. The green button is for advice on what it feels like to be about to die. If it turns out you were mistaken, then apologise to the doctor, select a club, and get on with the game.

By the fourth hole, I'm wondering if the alarms also connect to an emergency psychiatrist. Every time I line up a shot, John Mater thinks of someone he knows I ought to talk to. He wants to be helpful for my sports book, and John himself came fourth in the first ever Australian board-riding contest. Is that a fact? A little further down the fairway (and sometimes less far even than that) he tells me his son skied moguls for Australia for ten years. He mentions Mick Withers, on the tee up ahead of us, a fellow FAG but also a member of the Australian water polo team at four successive Olympics. In the same group Jo Alagich played football against Manchester United, but (I later find out) he lost the programme (his name on the stapled centre page opposite George Best) when he forgot it on the roof of his car. In the foursome behind us, Frank O'Neill played rugby against the touring All Blacks, and Bernie O'Connor was a Davis Cup reserve.

This is psychological torture. I am surrounded by elite Australian sportsmen, and though past their prime they're still competing, and from nowhere I feel the onset of the Cringe. I start to believe that every Manly Friday after-noon golfer is a former grand champion, with a champion's winning mentality.

I am not playing well. I'm unnerved by the possibility that everyone in Australia, without exception, is someone or knows someone who's turned out for the country, and probably been to the Olympics. This means that every

Australian child sees from an early age that sporting greatness is achievable, and within an ordinary grasp. It's not just a dream, because Uncle Bruce or Auntie Sheila was in Moscow throwing the javelin in 1980. No big deal.

I had an Auntie Sheila. She played bridge on Tuesday evenings at 57 Westlecot Road.

I'm now playing worse. Even the birds are laughing at me. I can't see them but they're making extraordinary noises, quizzical, teeth-brushing, curious, then intermittent cheeps and resigned, downturned whistles. They're disappointed in me. I see a pair of yellow flashes, parrots in the trees, zoo birds in zoo trees. I'm a long way from home. More to the point, I'm a long way from the green.

Failure in golf can be finely calibrated, because that's the kind of sport it is. I'm heading for a score of eighteen Stableford points. For non-golfers, think of a number very near the bottom of a precisely adjusted scale, a mark low down on the measure between hero and zero. That is where I am, at a level corresponding almost exactly to an official golfing result of Absolute Rubbish. It's a ten-minute mile, a one-metre high jump, several degrees below freezing. It's seventy-five all out.

As a consolation, coming up the eighteenth fairway at the end of the afternoon, the Australia of Manly Golf Club transforms itself through a filter of late sunlight into a soft spreading orchard of saturated European green. The rays through trees on tended grass appeal to some instinctive sense of the ideal, and I realise I could quickly feel possessive of this little patch of Manly. This is where, on a vast new continent of yellows and reds, I might feel welcome and safe, if only I could keep my ball on the fairway.

I trudge inside. If there's anything more dispiriting than playing bad golf, it's talking about it afterwards in the clubhouse bar. In English golf clubs, the bar is where language goes to die, where familiar phrases are smugged to death with the complacency of Peter Alliss – 'He's in a spot of bother, I fancy.'

The FAGs, however, have mastered this part of the day. Every Friday John Mater makes a jovial speech, and he also gives out prizes. I don't expect to be involved. I've already handed over money at the bar, a fistful of bright Australian banknotes, beyond caring about the maths but sure I lost and I was right. John stands by the bar and to read the results he puts on his glasses, balancing them halfway down his nose. However tough anyone starts out in life, this reading through glasses and then peering up above the frames is an excellent way to finish erudite and kindly. Even John Mater. He interrupts a joke someone is telling but politely waits for the punchline,

That's very nice, nurse, but all I said was are my tests back yet?

He then reads out the list of winners collated by John Johns from behind his ringmaster's table. Every winner is an Australian, a cash prize for the day's overall best scorer, cash for closest to the pin, and more cash for fewest putts of the day. It then turns out I'm a winner after all. I've won the Bradman, and John chucks me a new golf ball, in its sharp little box.

The Bradman, I discover, is not a good prize to win. Don Bradman was the world's most effective cricketer, famously averaging slightly less than a hundred as a Test match batsman. Whatever the conditions, whoever the opposition, Bradman nearly always had the most hits. The Bradman is therefore awarded in Australian golf for the day's worst score. I do my best, smile, raise the golf ball meekly above my head.

The Cringe confirmed.

'You can come again!' John Mater says. Everyone laughs.

Golf is a simple game. There's a stick which hits a ball towards a hole. Grip it and rip it. Or it's the most fiendish sporting challenge ever devised by man. The next Friday afternoon, from the first tee, the fairway between bunkers and trees appears unfeasibly narrow, as if I'm looking through the wrong end of a telescope. After last week's horror show I feel everyone watching me, the current undisputed holder of the Bradman, and I veer abruptly towards the fiendish. This is not encouraging.

Every time we lose to Australia, in any sport, it's more than a national crisis. It's that, obviously it is, but it's also a personal crisis, and this sense of personal inferiority is clearly worse if I'm the one doing the losing. Out and exposed in Manly, no England teams are representing me. The idea was that I didn't need representation. I *am* me.

In the week since I was last on Manly's first tee, I've therefore been trying to improve my chances by unfair means. Practice. It makes perfect, see? I played a round at the public course, Manly-Warringah, and was given a starting time with two undergraduates from New South Wales University. As media students, they couldn't be expected to be fully awake, not on a Wednesday afternoon, so I beat them easily, but what's the fun in beating people who are less good than me, even if they're Australians?

One practice round wasn't enough to solve the problem, so I moved on to the library, an airy modern building at the heart of Manly between the Corso and the Oval. It has 30,000 members who borrow close to 400,000 items a year, and as well as the novels and stories of Ernest Hemingway, and magazines on cars and sport, the Manly library might be expected to stock some basic sports psychology to help me cope with pressure. And boost my self-belief. I had high hopes that expert psychological tweaking could overcome any limitations inherent in being me or being English.

The Manly library, however, seems reluctant to help anyone who can't help themselves. At first all I find is a small book with a big title: *Don't Sweat the Small Stuff for Men, Simple Ways to Minimise Stress in a Competitive World.* Sport is small stuff, I reckon, and I'm ripe for some user-friendly self-help. Until I read the first sentence – 'I want you to know, up front, that I share many of the same struggles that you do.'

Oh yeah? What would a best-selling American pop-psychologist know about the Cringe, a sporting inferiority complex shared by a generation of English people over two decades, about being the Bradman, humiliated at the Manly Golf Club by Australians? I need specialist literature, the strong stuff, and with the help of a librarian I eventually track it down: *Gold Minds, The Psychology of Winning in Sport.*

That's more like it. The author is Brian Miller, a former psychologist at the Australian Institute of Sport, and apparently there are three factors that contribute to sporting success – skill levels, physical preparation and mental training. If you've neglected the first two, the third is obviously the one that counts.

Brian immediately lets me down: 'It is not possible to prescribe a system of mental preparation that works for all athletes, all teams, or all sports.' When this is exactly what I'm looking for, and if possible before next Friday afternoon.

I concentrate on what Brian Miller thinks I *can* do, desperate for the winning advice he once gave to many of Australia's top competitors.

1. Visualise

Easy. Go round in sixty, shake Jack Nicklaus by the hand (he's wearing 1970s check golfing trousers), get invited to the Masters, win the Green Jacket, retire and gloat for many years as a veranda member of Manly Golf Club.

2. Don't catastrophise

This is when one mistake means everything goes. I hit the ball into trees and I should never have been born. Don't do it. In fact, if you do it again, your life won't be worth living.

3. Memorise these catchphrases

'If not you then who?' John Mater and Steve Moran and Richard Clark and Bruce Jackson and Peter Haynes and Rob Ellis and Brian Fitzgerald and Bernie O'Connor and Nic Soglanich and Geoffrey Yonge and Frank O'Neill and John Maclean and Joe Alagich. All of Manly Golf Club.

'If not now then when?' Next Friday? Or maybe the one after that. Whenever.

'If it's to be, it's up to me!' I recite this to myself on the first tee, twitching my driver, feeling like a manic US teenager with metal teeth. The secret of golf is to empty your mind, only it's not much of a secret because everyone knows it. The secret is how best to achieve this, especially if you have a mind resistant to being emptied.

I swing back my driver (slowly, *slowly!*) but my mind is occupied with a question of faith and whether, like some committee member from the Imperial Bowling Board in 1905, I believe only the British are competent to play and win at sport. I swing down. I've not emptied my mind, stayed in the present. No great wonder then that my next shot is a five iron from the rough beside the lady's tee. Concentrate, swing back slowly, stay in the present while bearing in mind I have no right to play better because the game was developed on the island where I was born, like expecting a modern Dane to have a talent for knocking up a longship. A shank, behind a paperbark tree. I'm not even a hundred metres towards the first pin. It gets worse.

This next shot I'm going to bend low round a tree trunk with a seven iron, but I'm wondering whether the national disappointment we feel at losing, at any sport, must have in it some indulgent suspicion of a stolen birthright.

And so it goes on. Running up a huge score, a typically effortless century for the Bradman, I lose myself some-where between the backswing and the strike, thinking that wherever the British went pasteurising the planet of the 1800s they destroyed the local games. It's worth remembering this the next time you hear the gloat of little England about the many global sports we invented. Our games didn't take over the world because they were intrinsically better, but because we the British people who played them were everywhere. Our enthusiasm for rules and governing bodies made sport international, but before we arrived there were other sporting traditions we preferred to ignore.

In Australia, early settlers recorded an Aboriginal ball game in which the leathery scrotum of a kangaroo was stuffed with grass, greased, and used as a handball. It was a kind of piggy-in-the-middle with two teams of between fifty and a hundred competitors, and could be played for hours on end. The British authorities, officers and clergy, took a close look. Regretfully, it seemed like a free-for-all. There were no clear-cut rules or infringements. Even more baffling, it had no obvious moral value, a game played exclusively for fun.

Wherever Aborigines were allowed to congregate in any number, they showed a rare talent for the imported British sports. An Aboriginal cricket team toured England in 1868, and in 1893, once more against the English, Jack Marsh bowled his way to figures of 5 for 5 on behalf of New South Wales. The white Australians were unmoved. Jack Marsh was kept out of the Ashes team by his colour, and later battered to death in a street in Orange. His white assailants were cleared by a jury.

The Aborigines were so good at sport that spurious reasons were contrived to stop them taking part. They lacked moral character or intelligence, or were overly vulnerable to white vices, specifically alcohol. It was therefore a kindness to keep them away from holiday bats and balls. When these excuses became untenable, the Amateur Athletic Association devised an ingenious ruse. Aboriginal people were classified as professionals, all of them, in perpetuity. This meant they were automatically barred from the majority of sporting events, which were exclusively amateur. The administrators no doubt frowned and were sympathetic as they explained, palms held out and with a hopeless sigh, that they were sorry but they didn't make the rules.

Exiled to the professional circuit, on a training diet of 'tobacco and plenty of sherry', Charlie Samuels from Queensland ran the hundred yards in 9.1 seconds. Bobby Macdonald invented the crouch start for sprinters. The Aborigines could do what we did, seemingly without any great trouble. Could we do what they did?

Using knowledge passed from generation to generation, the Aboriginal tribes prospered for 60,000 years in the hostile natural habitat of Australia, home to more organic poisons than any other land mass on earth. That kind of survival would be a lot more manly, in Manly, than hitting a small white ball with a stick.

Dad taught me off breaks in the garden, and how to swing a golf club against a used car-tyre, but we never went camping. As an adult, I tried to repair this parental neglect by going camping at least once a year, five or six years in a row, with my friend Drew, who worked as an engineer on the cross-Channel ferries. The idea, or at least my idea, was that it was worth remembering on an annual basis how it felt to live without a roof.

Now I can't remember how it felt. Trying to recall that mixed sensation of vulnerability and freedom, I hit cover drives and pulls and all Bradman's favourite shots into the rough and bother of beyond the boundaries. At the par three eighth I then hit a perfect strike, perfectly directed in line with the pin, but with the wrong club and over the green and into the lake.

At the ninth tee, a sign warns golfers that plastic snakes have been placed on the green. The snakes frighten the cockatoos ('They'll eat your house,' Bernie explains.), but the sign isn't there in case golfers see a snake, mistake it for a real one, and then collapse from a heart attack (no emergency alarm on the ninth). Manly Golf Club has been here too long for that. It's to prepare the golfer for disappointment when a neat chip-and-run deflects from a plastic toy.

The FAGs throw the rubber cobras and plastic red-bellies off the greens, the groundsmen go round putting them back again, and although I'd be better occupied visualising the break of my delicate left-to-right putt, I console myself with the unmanliness of this pursuit. I think, despite the danger of real snakes and spiders, I should test myself against what the men of Manly were doing before we brought them the substitute of balls and sticks and whitewash, and imposed the tricky ninth green on their most sacred of cultural sites.

Sport is now a feature of the Australian landscape. There are over 1,500 golf courses, and at roughly 150 hectares per course, golf has colonised, let's say, 225,000 hectares of the country. Add to that the tens of thousands of football pitches and cricket ovals and swimming pools, and because Australia is so huge, it hardly makes a dent. The old landscape survives.

There's nowhere to camp legally within the civic boundaries of Manly, but I've no automatic objection to rules (I like sport), so I decide to go camping at the nearest place it's allowed. This is at a campsite called the Basin in Ku-ring-gai Chase National Park, fifteen hundred hectares of sandstone bushland only seventeen kilometres from Manly Corso.

Out of season, I'm the only passenger on the small ferry puttering across Pittwater from the jetty at Palm Beach. As I stand at the prow of the boat, feet apart and side-on like a parody of an adventurer, I feel horribly underprepared. I have a tent and a sleeping bag borrowed from Maria Silva; I also have convict food for added authenticity, bread and dried strings of meat. It doesn't seem much as the ferry eases its way up the Basin inlet, the forested slopes on each steep side of the river valley dark, quiet, too quiet.

It's about now that I recognise the stupidity of sleeping outside alone in the middle of 1,500 hectares of yet-to-be-developed golf course. I haven't brought enough food and I haven't read up on the wildlife. This makes me swallow hard and regret the many sensible precautions that I and thousands of other newcomers to Australia have traditionally overlooked, such as avoiding a life of crime in the late eighteenth century. Other neglected options include staying at home with my mum, ignoring the Assisted Passage Scheme, and rejecting all thoughts of a new life and enlightenment.

Before setting out I did manage to ask wise old Jack Astley from the rifle club for any tips he might have on bush walking and camping. This seemed like a good use of Jack's key preparation window, the last minute, especially as Jack can trace his mother's side of the family back to the First Fleet – the ramshackle flotilla of eleven ships that first made land in Australia. Jack thought for a second.

'Goannas,' he said. 'Big monitor lizards as long as your leg. Don't get between a goanna and its tree.'

This, Jack explained, is because a startled goanna makes a run for its tree. If you get in the way, the lizard thinks you're the tree trunk and climbs up you instead.

'They have nails as long as your finger,' Jack said mildly, perhaps even cheerfully. 'They'll rip you to shreds.'

Thanks, Jack.

'You should be all right for snakes and spiders. It's not their time of year.'

'Well, that's something.'

'Though you can't be too careful.'

The Basin campsite is a wide expanse of flat ground at the edge of a lagoon, with a yellow fringe of beach between the two. As the ferry moves away, I introduce myself to the ranger and pick a spot for my tent, which is more difficult than it might be because there's no one else here. I can choose any pitch I like on this flat stretch of land tamed from the bush, with short cropped grass, and that's how I like it, tamed. I say goodbye to the ranger, twice, but he doesn't attempt to hold me back and keep me safe. He tells me to enjoy my day's walking, and expects that as a tourist from England I'll enjoy the exotic wildlife: goannas and wallabies and highly toxic snakes.

'Sure,' I say. 'I will. Thanks.'

Of course I want to see wildlife. But also I don't. I yomp as noisily as I can, stamping on the steep tracks, cracking twigs, dislodging rocks, enjoying an out-loud conversation about why so few of the Australians I've met have mentioned the upcoming Ashes series. Perhaps they're kinder than I expected, more restrained and considerate.

Near the end of the first track there's an Aboriginal engraving site, and when I get there I meet sixty schoolchildren from St Agatha's Primary School, Pennant Hills. This is what it says on their royal-blue sweatshirts. They also have blue shorts, long grey socks and blue floppy hats, a very quiet pack of six-year-old Australian Catholics with ochre smeared whitely in lines across their cheeks. The adult guide is telling them how in the old days life used to be simpler; and he's right, at the beginning it was simple enough. As Captain Cook himself said, 'all they seemed to want was for us to be gone'. When keen British linguists eventually deciphered the Manly Gurringai language, they searched back for the first recorded words spoken to Europeans. Translated, they meant, 'Go away.'

The engravings on the flat sandstone rocks are rudimentary whales and some hand-prints. In truth, there's not much to see, and this was always part of the trouble.

The Aboriginal people didn't have impressive possessions or relics. They had no houses or obvious hierarchies ruled by corruptible kings, like the immediately magnificent Tahitians and Maoris. Instead of a culture the British could understand and manipulate, the Aborigines had stories.

I follow the dry red roads through the scrubland of scribbly gums and bloodwood trees. I come across a pair of sea eagles, and a stroppy German teenager made to go fishing with her parents. It's almost as I expected Australia to look back in the days when we were digging for it, like Rolf Harris used to paint it on Saturday afternoon *Cartoon Time*. A bit of blue (doobie-do) a touch of red here (der-doing, der-doing), BIG splash of yella (uh-huh, uh-huh) a few glints of white and there you go, mate. That's pretty much what the Ku-ring-gai Chase National Park looks like on a sunny winter's day.

Every time I go hiking I imagine that I'm going to have the space and solitude, and inclination, to think great thoughts and resolve the conundrum of the universe. In fact, I never think of anything much at all, apart from not breaking my legs, making progress, seeing and forgetting and seeing again. I enter the perfect state of mind, of alert emptiness, for playing golf. What a waste.

In Ku-ring-gai Chase there's a small settlement at a place called Mackerel Bay. A footpath marked on the map has been blocked off by residents with a sign saying 'Private Property Keep Out'. I have to make a wide detour and only just make it back into camp by six. It is dark, or very nearly. A four-wheel drive draws up from behind the toilet block, which is closed for the winter. It's the ranger, one hand on the steering wheel, elbow out the window.

'Good walk?'

'Great, thanks.'

'Watch out for the bandicoots. They get hungry. See ya.'

And he drives off. No new tents have been set up; I'm quite alone. I whistle. I hum and ha. I wish I knew what a bandicoot was. Then I look on the bright side: I won't have to accept offers of help if I get into trouble. Darkness has by now closed in, at which point I learn a valuable lesson, one that I'm about to pass on for everyone's benefit.

Went bush walking in Australia and didn't see any wildlife? Not a problem. Hang around. Stay the night. The wildlife will come to you. I turn on the torch to get to my tent, and everywhere there are black swamp wallabies indifferent to a lone night-time camper. They hunch over interesting patches of dinner grass, and hop lazily from one to the next.

I snatch up my convict rations and carry them jealously to the end of the wooden wharf, where I sit and eat under a single electric bulb. I'm as far as I can get from the humming and clicking forest, water slapping against the white struts of the wharf, slick like oil where I can see it through the slats in the decking. Moths are flitting about, and in the distance I can see the flash of the lighthouse at Barrenjoey Point. Out on the wharf I feel adventurous and safe like a contestant on reality TV but without the TV, and looking up I discover no cheeky Union flag in the left-hand corner of the starry southern sky.

I'm still hungry. No matter, I can make some fishing lines from the fibrous bark of a cabbage-tree palm, and hooks from limpet shells. I'll strengthen the line by soaking it in a solution from the sodden bark of a geebung. Pound it, roll together two strands of the fibre, then immerse in the sap of the red bloodwood to prevent fraying. As a staple, a side dish, I'll eat the fish I catch with the seed of the burrawang, which is bright orange, but also full of starch and poison.

If I needed to do this to survive, I'd be dead.

Unable to tell my geebungs from my burrawangs, I climb into the tent at seven. The bandicoots make their first attack at ten, but I tell myself not to be scared of small furry mammals. At least they're small. But numerous. I'm scared, and make an unseemly to-do of seeing off all-comers whatever they are with a brave stumble round the tent and a strafing torch and over-expressive hand-waving. All is suddenly calm. Under the broad night sky I stand and think wistfully of the solid buildings of Manly, a fringe idea, a small outpost on the edge. The national park, on the other hand, even so close to the city and the sea, heaves with the organic glamour of the interior.

It suddenly seems possible that two centuries of settlement are irrelevant, and that the night and the bush and the creatures will prevail again soon, by natural law. This seems no more fanciful than the idea of cursed Australian golfers. Or the notion that a lizard god created the mountains and hills directed by a supreme being named Baiame and his one-legged son, the mischievous and sometimes vindictive Daramulan. Outside alone at night, none of these ideas seem strained.

I have another fend at the bandicoots, who are surprisingly game, but I'm less scared now that I know what they look like. Somewhere between a rat and an anteater, though not so big as either. And they're naturally scared of me, or they ought to be, because for 60,000 years the Aborigines killed bandicoots, ate bandicoots, used bandicoot bones as hole-punches and needles, and adapted bandicoot skins for a cooking method now better known as boil-in-the-bag.

When they get too close, this is what I shout at them: 'Boil-in-the-bag! Boil-in-the-bag!' They scarper. The bandicoots and I, I think we're beginning to understand each other.

What really scares people, and by people I mean me, is people. Like the one community in Ku-ring-gai Chase blocking its rights of way with 'Private Property Keep Out'. The signs might as well read 'Private Property We Are Very Frightened'. And therefore best to keep out, because frightened people are dangerous, like the ragged 1,400 of the disembarked First Fleet. In their defence, they must have been frightened witless.

I didn't have a bad night, all things considered, because we're a tough bunch, us human beings. That's how a group of strangers can sail 15,900 miles to an unknown continent without one person on board knowing how to farm, and end up 200 years later with a nation of twenty million people eating kebabs on shopping streets named after the highways of Rome. People are tough, only these days we don't get so many chances to prove it. That's partly what sport is for. It means you don't have to go camping. Or colonising.

Distracted by long-nosed bandicoots and the Ku-ring-gai Chase National Park, not living in the present and empty-ing my mind, another Friday afternoon of golf is ruined.

At the tenth, I hit my tee shot twice out of bounds, then vent my frustration by pretending to mark my card but in fact blunting my golf pencil in a scrawl of 'DAMN! FUCK DAMN!' as the only way of just about keeping a lid on it. I take a long, hard look at myself, and start wondering what I'm good at. What *are* you good at? As a writer, my handicap is about three or four, but I sometimes play lower than that. As a golfer, I remind myself I'm here to write a book, wanting to be good at something else because against Manly Australians I'm so obviously useless at golf. This is a delusion, a deception. Right now on the golf course, all I want to be good at is golf.

At the next hole, my pencil increasingly stubbed and black, I block my approach, pick up my ball and mark my score – 'FUCKITY FUCKITY CRAP'. Not great for my writer's handicap, but as an anger-management technique it seems to help. A little.

Nationality seems irrelevant. On this form I could lose to anyone from anywhere in the world, because golf is a test of individual character that I'm failing. If nationality could help, it would cut in like a superhero's secret power, the ability to jump like a spider or hear like a bat, a quality to own and exploit that never actually has to be earned. It's just there, and will reveal itself in moments of competitive stress. This is a more consoling thought for Australians than for the English.

Losing to Australians at golf would be easier to bear if the FAGs were sporting obsessives, Dennis Lillee clones with aggressive facial hair and a habitual snarl of triumph. This Friday I'm being beaten by Peter Haynes, a stamp collector. Mostly, he's interested in the colonial period. I'm also being beaten by Bruce Jackson, a farmer wearing knee-length shorts and long woollen socks.

At the halfway house between holes eleven and twelve, while the others stop for soup and a pie, I try to patch up my self-esteem by giving myself a good talking-to in the Gents. As a visitor I go round the back of the hut and through the first door I see, marked 'Associates', assuming this means non-members. It's the Ladies. Men are

Members, the next door along. I try to resist all sorts of excuses for falling to pieces, the heat, the away fixture, my lack of practice, the Cringe. But I'm still falling to pieces, and I feel sorry for people who take golf seriously. Like me. Right now. I backed myself (mate), and I lost.

Golf has no mercy, unlike bowls. If you lose badly at bowls the match finishes reasonably quickly, in as little as an hour and a half. Go and have a drink and forget about it. Golf makes you suffer right to the end, over the full four hours and eighteen holes, however dreadfully you play. And today it's so bad that by the finishing stretch I'm playing for my pride, as the saying goes.

As I trudge up the eighteenth fairway towards the white and glimmering clubhouse, my score is fifteen. For those still unclear about the Stableford system, this dips lower on my universal quality scale than Absolute Rubbish. I am a wretch (I am catastrophising). I am diminished in defeat, and not the man I'd hoped to be, as recently as this morning. Must have aimed too high, and I've been cut down to size for wanting to be the best man, because the best man wins, and defeat now confirms my worst opinion of myself, an incompetent, an Englishman, a crumbling sandstone.

Another discouraging day for British sport, and the worst is yet to come. Peter Haynes, the stamp collector, must have managed a glance at my X-rated scorecard. I then lift my ball inch-perfectly into the centre of the bunker in front of the eighteenth green. That's when Peter says it. He puts his hand on my shoulder and walks me up to the sand. We look at my ball, plugged.

'Never mind, Richard,' he says. 'It's only a game.'

When you hear those words, all is lost. That's the sign, if you've ever wondered, that you were playing for your pride and you lost, and I, and I, I look around in a rage and decide it probably doesn't matter if I can still physically beat up the rest of the four-ball. I glare at them, sturdy, healthy, happy, good at golf. I'm not convinced I could, not even if I take them one at a time.

At the presentations, for the second week in a row, I win the Bradman. John Mater, glasses halfway down his nose, tosses me a ball in its box and introduces me once again, 'all the way from England . . .' Not even John can make a joke of this one. I've played so badly that the farmer and yacht racer Bruce Jackson buys me a drink and tells me, in a friendly way, that he thinks I'm involved in some kind of elaborate scam. Apparently, as well as being rubbish at golf, I don't take enough notes.

'I've got a good memory,' I say (*that nine iron at the eighth!*).

'It doesn't add up. I think you're a con man.'

I try to imagine a con man so smooth he talks his way into exclusive Group One golf clubs, where he proceeds to lose his pride, and his money. He must really love the game of golf, this con artist, but perhaps he was black-balled everywhere else for repeatedly marking his scorecard 'CRAPPING HELL!' when he should have been recording his partner's number of putts.

There's nothing else for it. To compete I shall have to cheat. Or adjust my handicap, which among golfers may amount to the same thing. As I stride onto the tee for the third Friday in a row I announce my handicap as twenty-seven. I place the ball on the tee and I whack it, because off twenty-seven no one is expecting miracles. Of course it flies straight and true, right down the middle of the fairway, and from then on everything is fine and dandy. Golf is so much easier when you're not under pressure, and if I can only keep my handicap high enough, I'll win the important matches every time.

This unique and useful feature of golf is also its central deception. Handicapping means I can beat someone who's better than me, though he's still better than me, even on the day. We both know that, and handicapping is a lie at the heart of the game, an accommodation. It patronises the less skilful players and gives golf that shimmer of phoniness as certain around golf courses as drains. Half the players at any given time are usually being supercilious to the other half, simply by pretending they're equals.

I don't know whether golf develops character, but it certainly finds the extremes of the character anyone already has. I hit a few good shots and I'm charming, and chat away cogently to my partners about the ongoing business that attaches itself to sports clubs everywhere. There's a plan to add more water to the course, but is change for the better? A local resident has complained because she saw a man urinating by the lake, and there's some background controversy about a car-park development.

When I've hit a particularly sweet approach, I ask the other players why it is that 1.4 million Australians play golf every year, but they don't have a champion. Everyone points out, knowing the statistic by heart, that there are five Australians in the top fifty, but it's true there's no world-beater, and world-beating is what Australians do best. We reach a consensus where Australian golfers seem to be lacking in some essential mental rigour. I like that conclusion.

'Now New Zealanders, they're competitive,' someone says, as if it was a competition. 'Especially the women.'

I'm interested to find out if the Friday afternoon golfers feel they get more competitive as they age, maybe because there's less time left to make amends for a howler into the trees. I'll have to wait until I get old to find out, because nobody in the FAGs understands the question. There's not one of them who sees himself as old.

Instead, they keep alive the boy culture, right to the end, putting grass in each other's drinks and standing on each other's tee pegs and joshing about senior moments. This is when they forget someone's name, or whether their down swing is a practice or for real, leading to a disastrous last minute lunge for the ball.

The Manly Friday afternoon golfers are like a large squad of retired cricketers, decent-hearted men making a team game out of a mean sport, at ease with themselves even as they unconsciously echo, every Friday afternoon, the ancient patterns of Australia. The Aborigines prefer to walk the country in groups, mixing young and old. Knowledge about the landscape, its threats and rewards, is passed down from generation to generation – 'You want to keep to the right here' – and every creek, headland and promontory has a name, even if at Manly it's only holes one to eighteen.

Then I have a run of bad shots and I can't even speak.

The trouble with golf is that when I get it wrong, I'm useless, but if I get it right, I'm not suddenly a supreme being. I'm about par for the course, and I'd no more congratulate myself for being good at walking, or drinking liquids. A good shot is never lucky, because that was always the intention. Even a perfect shot isn't lucky, because that's what I visualised beforehand.

All the same, I play some incredibly lucky shots, when the ball goes precisely where I intended. To make this kind

of luck contractual, I devise increasingly paranoid super-
stitions. I'll do anything to keep my game in order, from
wearing odd socks to eating half my scoring pencil. I must
have no coins in my pockets and only five tees, three of
which must be white and made of wood. I'll do anything
to win, but the sense I need something else, apart from
and in addition to the pure will to win (and exaggerating
my handicap), suggests that I'm not a winner.

Peter May was given the England cricket captaincy aged
twenty-five with the sole objective of beating the
Australians. Before he made it to thirty, he was hag-ridden
by stomach ulcers, an English body catastrophised. It
could be that sport and winning just isn't that important.
Kick back. Let it go. Enjoy yourself.

Third Test

*The risk and danger attached to surf-bathing is the very
spice of it and only helps to make our young men manly
and hardy and probably teaches them to have some
presence of mind in emergency.*

Sydney Morning Herald, 1907

I should banish the Cringe not by struggling to beat the
Australians, but by being less English about losing. So
we're rubbish at cricket and tennis; I can't beat anyone at
golf, but so what? This is Australia, and the sun will shine
tomorrow. Hit the beach, work on the tan, watch the
pretty Manly girls go by.

I come from a very small island, but I've never lived by
the sea. Down on the ocean beach at Manly, this seems a
dreadful omission. It's winter, but there are Manly people
sunbathing and barefoot soft-sand jogging. Out in the
waves, in black wetsuits, muscled surfers swoop and drop,
glistening in the winter sunshine. Taking it easy, not
being competitive, I fetch a cappuccino from a coffee
shop over the road, find an empty bench on the
promenade.

At Manly, the beach is a layered experience. First there's the ocean, and no Australian makes the mistake of calling the Pacific the sea. Sea is too feeble a word, too weedy, which explains why there's no such thing as oceanweed. After the ocean comes the beach, and after the beach the most recent and reticent layer, the promenade, where I am now. The promenade is raised above the beach for about a kilometre and a half, all the way from Manly Life Saving Club at the south end to Queenscliff Surf Life Saving Club at the north. The North Steyne Surf Life Saving Club is in the middle. Basically, on Manly beach your life is in safe hands; even safer if you stay fully dressed and sit drinking coffee on the promenade, shaded from the sun by an avenue of Norfolk Island pines, the trees that caused the British Empire so much trouble.

Norfolk Island is 1,610 kilometres east-north-east of Sydney – eight kilometres long, five kilometres wide, and one of the main reasons Britain wanted the Union flag flying in Australia. Blame the trees. Captain Cook had seen the Norfolk pines on his way past in 1774. Three feet in diameter and 180 feet high, they looked perfect for the masts and spars always in demand by a British navy ordained to rule the waves. As it happened, Norfolk Island pines were short-grained and low in resin. They snapped like bone. By the time this became clear, the British were already installed on an unwelcoming, unproductive rock in the middle of the Pacific. No one wanted to go there. Naturally, as the last and worst place in the world, it became the destination for Sydney recidivists.

Norfolk Island was the place of ultimate terror, what Robert Hughes evocatively calls a 'kakotopia'. There was no hope of reform or redemption. There was quarrying, flogging on suspicion, underwater rock-breaking, solitary confinement, male rape. The minimum sentence was ten years.

On the other hand, a century later, the trees were found to flourish and provide cool green shadow for amblers on Manly's ocean-front promenade. Australia's colonial history is young and supple. It takes in chain gangs clanking in their 'canaries', the first national strip made of coarse wool in yellow and grey. Almost at the same time, considering the long reach of history, it takes in Lycra power-walkers and power-prammers shaded by the same pines, joggers in sunglasses, and bodies at play in the surf and sand as they have been since 1903, when Manly invented beach culture.

Until then, anyone who wanted to expose any part of their body to a person of the opposite sex had to do it at night, after dark. This included swimming. A newspaper editor, William Gocher of the *Manly and North Sydney News*, publicly defied the daylight bathing ban on three successive Sundays in September 1902 at Manly Beach. Or at least he said he did. He was a journalist, and it may have been someone else. In any case, the by-law was rescinded a year later and from November 1903 the Manly ferries were packed with Sydneysiders eager to expose their bodies in daylight. This fad quickly spread to the rest of Australia's beaches until, as John Pilger writes, 'we found our freedom by taking our clothes off and doing nothing of significance, and by over the years refining and elevating this state of idleness to a "culture" now regarded highly in the world's most fashionable places'.

If the beach has a culture, then surfing is its heavenly music. On the sand, boards under their arms, surfers always run. It's as if once they've made up their minds, they just have to get out there and surf, riding the frontier between ocean and beach.

How hard can it be? I suspect the secret of surfing is that it's easier than it looks, otherwise fewer people would do it. As easy as buying a VW camper van after a discussion in a pub agreeing that MOTs are overrated.

Up at the golf club, one of the jolly old red-faced boys once said, 'Write about me. I was the best surfer ever.'

'Really?'

'Yeah. I just liked to keep a low profile.'

Surfing in their day was non-competitive, and therefore a bit of a joke. Up at the golf club, sport means the record, the score, the winners and losers taken down as evidence in John Johns's ledgers on the table. It's the Australian way.

It's also an approach I'm trying to avoid, for mental health reasons, but within an hour, telling myself this is fine because surfing is a non-organised, non-competitive sport, I find that it's me, a plank, the Pacific Ocean.

There can only be one winner.

And that winner is the plank. Made of polyurethane and fibreglass, it will float without biodegrading for the next 15,000 years, by which time the Pacific will have dried up from climate change caused by the exhaust emissions from unroadworthy VW camper vans. I will be long dead.

Even, I soon realise, a little longer dead than originally planned. Surfing is not easier than it looks. I never really recover from the moment it dawns on me, wet, exhausted, and beginning to feel the cold, that indie rock music will not blast from the sky the first time I catch a wave. What I do hear, as I tumble about underwater, working out the biomechanical principles of inverted wave-riding, is a blond-haired Australian dude laughing and shouting 'Rip it up, Rich!'

Mike 'Froth' Taylor, surf instructor, thirty-two years old going on twenty, is the most positive man alive. He works for Manly Surf School, which has a rare licence to operate from the beach, using the basement of the North Steyne Surf Life Saving Club as office, storeroom and general headquarters. The basement is full of boards and not much else, like a garage opening directly on to the sand.

I sign up with Mike for an adults-only lesson, to avoid the embarrassment of being shown up by children, most probably Australian. It seems to make sense. I'm in my late thirties. I'm an adult. But when Mike gathers together the adults-only beginners' group on the beach in front of the surf school, I can't believe it. *I'm* an adult, I am, but they're letting in adults who are only nineteen or twenty years old.

The only other genuine old-timer is Chris, a local in his mid-thirties and a New South Wales state swimmer. He thought it was about time he had a go and, like me, he has to get his surfing in now. In five years time neither of us will be bending at the knee. And we can't do it when we're twenty, when we'd have cinched it, because we didn't.

The first problem is the wetsuit. I've never worn a wetsuit before, and I need a lesson in putting on wetsuits before I have a lesson in surfing.

Then I discover there's hard work to be done long before the yee-ha indie three-chord romp. There's warming up, dragging the board along the beach, the battle of the paddle-out, and then the submerged white flywheel on the way back in.

With skiing, I'm usually encouraged by the feeling that

the mountain wants me to go down it. If on an Alp I do nothing, and relax, that's what will probably happen. I'm not so sure the wave wants me on it, whatever Mike says. If I do nothing and relax, I will drown.

'Hey, Mike,' I say, coming up for air after another double rinse and spin, 'was that good?'

'Mate!' sunshine Mike says, pushing himself up on his board and hooting, 'Whoo! It's *all* good!'

Mike surfs every day except when his back plays up, a repetitive strain injury from surfing since the age of thirteen. It's the most common surfer's complaint, but otherwise, Mike says, it's a low-impact sport and you can go on for years, catching fifteen waves an hour, twenty max, and standing up for between five and ten seconds a shout.

He makes it sound a breeze, which it isn't, but even though I'm having trouble standing up, and I'm not competitive, I'm still the winner because the best surfer is the one having the most fun. That's what Mike says. And I'm having a lot of fun: I'm covered for liability insurance, I've got a soft board, and I have no idea what I'm doing or how dangerous it is. Even when I'm not having fun, underwater and smashed to bits with a plastic fin in my ear, the thought of how much fun surfing could one day become overrides how much fun it actually is. Though come to think of it, the same applies to golf.

While we're dragging our boards back to the shed, we're intercepted by a twin-pair of twelve-year-old girls with their dad. They're undecided for about half a second before Mike has them hooked. 'We'll go out the back, do the white water, whatever, you're gonna *love* it!' And after they disappear, all hopped up on Mike's enthusiasm, I ask him who makes the best learners and of course it's kids, the lucky buggers, up to about the age of fourteen, due to the board-to-body ratio. Basically, they're standing on a door, a deck, and the wave just sweeps them in.

'Girls,' Mike says. 'They can take a bigger beating and come straight back out.'

'What about English people?' Sometimes you just have to prompt.

Mike doesn't want to say it, but I can be quite insistent on this subject. English people. The pale guys stuck at 'Before' in bodybuilding's 'Before' and 'After'. Or if they get to 'After', beer-idiots who know it all already, so don't need lessons at anything, and who are you calling an idiot? I think that about covers us. 'What are the English like as surf learners?'

'Mate.' Mike is torn between not wanting to be negative and telling me the truth. 'Whoo! Rock on! They have no motorskills and underdeveloped muscle groups. The English women are physically weak.'

'Oh.'

He thinks that about covers us.

'Buddy! Cheer up, mate! It's not like it's the Ashes! Same time tomorrow?'

I retreat to the promenade, and watch people doing nothing, but they're tanned and glistening as if they've just finished a long and energising something. Haunted by a past life spent mostly indoors, I wonder where all these people are supposed to be. I see a very brown man with a shock of white hair walking backwards. He's wearing dark blue trunks with *MANLY* across the buttocks and waving at people as he passes. He must be about sixty. He should be at work.

I lie down on a bench in the foetal position, too tired to cross the road for a coffee and a huge bun, which I quite fancy. Instead I look side-on across the beach and console myself with metaphors for life provided by the infinite Pacific. Swim with the current. Go with the flow. Most importantly of all, when a rip begins to drag you out, don't try to fight it.

My eyes are the only part of my body not stiffening up, and their male gaze works like a surf movie. Focus on the waves, study some radical moves, glance and linger on some solid pecs or a nice bum in a bikini. Repeat. Throughout this loop, I have a nagging sense that Australians are simply luckier than us. They live on the peaceful side of the world where the sun always shines. They have sand and sea, and no hereditary peerage. All the teenagers have fantastic sex whenever they fancy it, and the first time, so it's said, is more likely than not on a beach.

If there are parallel lives and universes, where everything turns out differently, then for many English people this is one. For anyone born between about 1940 and 1982, this could easily have been you, mate. I could have been the Australian I set out to beat, one of the million and a half Britons who arrived in Australia between 1947 and 1982 in one of the largest planned migrations in history. It was called the Assisted Passage Scheme.

The migrants paid ten quid, surrendered their passports, and promised to refund the full fare if they bottled it and went back home within two years. Eighty-four per cent of them were English, and here at Manly is the blue and gold lifestyle most of them were hoping to find when they got here, on the far side of the mirror, at the other end of the earth.

Manly Beach was used to illustrate the Department of Immigration's official brochure, which had the no-frills title 'Emigrate to Australia for £10'. In a panel called *Australia's Famous Climate*, a portly Dad is running barefoot through the shallows at Manly holding hands with two young children. The square sandstone blocks of St Patrick's are clearly visible on the North Head skyline in the background.

Manly was what the English immigrants were promised.

Manly Beach and endless sport in the sunshine. Applications surged after the 1956 Melbourne Olympics – for the sun and the sport, naturally, but also for the avoidance of European nuclear meltdown. The Commonwealth Games from Perth were a televised glimpse of heaven during a terrible British winter in 1962–3, and the '60s were the peak period for emigration, over 80,000 British people fed up with Britain in 1969 alone.

So why not my mum and dad, like so many others, with a young family and hope for a better future? We lived in the area most emigrants came from, the south of England, and Dad was in the right kind of trade, building. Billboard adverts commissioned by the Australian government plastered English provincial towns, and their bright beachy optimism must have influenced generations of children, even those who can't now remember what they said. *Walk Tall in Australia*. At the beginning, the pitch was simple: *Sun and Meat*. Later, *There's a Man's Job for you in Australia*.

Always: *A Better Life for the Kids*.

No wonder it was easy, as an adult, to believe they were better than us. That's what they'd always been saying, loudly and in public on posters as big as a bus, so why didn't we give in at the time? Why not us? Why not me?

Probably, I think, because we weren't a family of swimmers.

Even in the winter, there can be no excuse for living in Manly and not learning to swim like a fish. In England, the grey waters off Lyme Regis make non-swimming a reasonable decision. The North Sea around Cromer is another national justification, as used to be the old and cracked pool at the Milton Road Baths in Swindon, where we went on Saturday mornings with Dad to give Mum a break. Seeing as Dad himself couldn't swim, we didn't get much encouragement to abandon the shallow end. Sport, it wasn't.

Manly is founded on swimming. Dick Cavill invented the Australian crawl in the Lavender Bay baths in Sydney, and then took the Manly ferry to demonstrate the efficiency of his new stroke in the ocean breakers. Before very long, fearless Australian youngsters were enthusiastically coming to Manly to drown.

In my own history of swimming, I preferred the new Oasis Leisure Centre to the Milton Road baths. The pool there had multicoloured slides and a wave machine, so you could have a fun splash and giggle without having to learn a swimming stroke. Before I knew it, not swimming because there wasn't a decent pool became avoiding decent pools because I couldn't swim. Not that I'm a non-swimmer, not strictly, just one of the world's worst swimmers amongst those who can stay afloat. I didn't want to drown as a surfer; it therefore made sense to know how to swim like an Australian.

First stop Manly Fishos, a sporting club that has a swimming section. It also has fishing and darts and hockey and golf and trivia, for the same reason that Gerry Muoio's North Manly Bowls Club has subsections for cricket, soccer and touch-rugby. The Austrian Club, along with shooting in its restaurant, has a soccer team. This is because in Australia, to get an alcohol licence, every club has to prove it's not a pub, and it can best do this by demonstrating the range of activities offered with membership. These are usually sporting, because sports are cheap and easy to organise. The Australian licensing laws have therefore made a direct contribution to Australia in glory on the podium.

Seeing as it isn't a pub, and that's official, the inside of the Manly Fishing and Sporting Association clubhouse looks very much like a pub. There is one large first-floor room full of glazed punters on bang-and-whistle fruit machines, and another large first-floor room empty except for some glazed punters at a basic rectangular table, seriously on the beer.

It's also like a pub in the sense that membership isn't designed to keep anyone out. It's not the golf club (first year membership £6,000) and the Fishos costs £5 a year, for which you get fruit machines, a window for the TAB nationalised betting tote, beer, occasional live music, more beer and Bobby Yonks. He's at the table of serious drinkers, big, hard-looking men with calluses on their hands and heads. Bobby Yonks has a peeling red face, dreadful teeth, a stutter, but there's a memory of kindness in his eye – a man who never forgets he loved his mother. By comparison I am medium-sized and soft as whipped cream, and my eye is perhaps less kindly. The receptionist who signed me in told me that Bobby Yonks would know about the swimming. I buy him beer, he buys me beer, but it takes a while to fit in because I'm suspected of being a spy from the developers.

'This place used to have a bad reputation for fighting,'

someone tells me, sizing me up. 'We had a lot of coconuts.'

'You mean mad people?'

'Islanders.'

There's baby-girl gymnastics on a huge screen showing only sport from the Foxtel subscription channel, and after a while everyone thaws as we drink too much and find a shared interest in traction engines.

At some point I learn that the swimming section of the Fishos only operates in summer, but big Bobby Yonks suggests I come along to the Frigid Frogs, a specialised winter swimming club. Whatever the weather, the Frogs swim every Sunday morning in the ocean pool at Curl Curl Beach.

'We have races,' Bobby says. 'Hur-hur. And we have drinking.'

'So I'd have to race?'

'Oh yes. Everyone has to race. Then we have a beer.' He starts chuckling. 'Or two.'

Typical, I think. I want to learn to crawl like an Australian, but before my first lesson I've already been offered a race. Maybe that's the best way to learn. I remind myself I'm not being competitive and say thanks, but no. Better learn to swim first, just in case.

But even thinking about swimming turns me to jelly. I ring up Manly's Boy Charlton Swim Centre and ask stupid questions over the phone, like do I need to bring a swim cap? This is because we had them when I was seven – white if you could swim a length, yellow for a width, red if you sank. It was a full-colour, full-detail panic flashback – I told my mum I'd earned a white cap and she rewarded me with the mask and flippers I wanted because they had them on the TV in *Barrier Reef*. She took the mask and flippers away again when she saw me in the pool on sports day, in a red cap, sinking.

Back in Manly, interrupting a fresh anxiety about goggles, I remember more importantly that I don't own any swimming trunks. Tight or baggy, long or short, plain or sporty or ironic?

My last failed swimming lesson (aged about twelve) was so long ago we listened to Blondie's 'Heart of Glass' in the school minibus on the way to the pool. Like Australia, school has infinite ways of finding winners and losers, and in those days the losers rolled their towels long and floppy. The winners made an extra fold before rolling, and had their towels stout and compact, like my towel now, and I don't know which is more pathetic, that I should remember this detail or that I should then take care to get my towel in the right shape, today, at my age, heading for the Boy Charlton Swim Centre in Manly.

How bad can this be? As bad as anyone's least favourite dream, stranded naked in front of strangers. But it's OK. I won't be naked. I have my new mirrored swimming goggles.

The Boy Charlton Swim Centre commemorates the 1924 Olympic swimming champion Boy Charlton. That was the Olympics when Manly provided all three gold medallists for Australia, in the triple jump, high diving and 1,500 metres swimming (seventeen-year-old Charlton one minute inside the world record). Not that I'm keeping score, not since the golf club, but the Cringe can sometimes seem like a correct response. Everywhere I go in Manly I'm in contact with sporting history and legends, and I'm not used to local heroes. Cronies of my dad, after a few pints, sometimes talk about Don Rogers, who scored for Swindon in the 1969 League Cup Final and had a sports shop on Faringdon Road. It's not the same somehow.

The swim teacher is from Northern Ireland, but this isn't how she says it. She says, 'I used to live in Northern Ireland.' Which is a pretty good solution. I try it on for size. 'I used to live in England. Now I'm Manly through and through.'

Meeting Australians who started off somewhere else is getting to be a habit, a full range of accents mocking the idea that Australians are born and bred differently, with an inherent ruthless winning streak. It's just the attitude that changes once you get here. Chance your arm because there's no home to hold you back, no hearth to encourage retreat. The Australian girl who used to live in Northern Ireland is braving a new life as a swim teacher, and I'm learning how to swim after thirty-eight years because in Australia I'm prepared to give it a shake.

Why it should be that simple, I don't know. Or I do: it's something I'm learning, and one factor is that I took a short walk, not even as far as the golf course or the twenty-four-hour tennis courts, and here I am undressed in the sunshine and staring at a flat blue Olympic fifty-metre swimming pool. If fifty metres is too daunting, then on the other side of the swim shop there's a second pool, half the size. I'm ready to have a go because I can.

My other sports aren't much help when it comes to swimming. In rugby, it's generally accepted that the opposition players always look bigger, irrespective of their actual size. In shooting, everyone else looks calmer, in bowls cannier, and in golf richer and more at ease. In swimming, the others look more buoyant.

I mustn't let that put me off, even if until now I've always done breaststroke, like serving underarm in tennis.

It works, and it's allowed, but nobody worth respecting is ever seen doing it. I want to swim freestyle, the Australian crawl.

The Northern Irish Australian shows me the basics. Breathe every three strokes, first one side and then the other. Oh, and breathe out underwater, which I never knew before. That explains a lot. Coordinate arms and legs. Now practise.

'Is that it?'

'I'd say so. Apart from the practice. Mind how you go, now.'

I say thank you, and goodbye, and while practising I make my second big discovery about freestyle swimming. It's hard work. I used to treat swimming as fun, the splash and giggle of the Oasis Leisure Centre. I never braced myself for the effort of all-in wrestling, and that's probably why I didn't make much progress. After sprinting the length of a rugby pitch, I wouldn't complain because I was out of breath, but swimming too is a gum-shield sport. Get fit. Get your head on. Swim.

The two lifeguards are wearing baggy shorts, white polo shirts and sunglasses under broad-brimmed sunhats. I know this because they're now, both of them, standing with their arms crossed at the end of my lane. I suppose that answers my question about how my new stroke must look. Relax. They're relaxed. Bubbles. Breathe. The light is silver and blue. Distance has no meaning, because everywhere is far away, especially the end of this fifty-metre lane. Runners have their distances, and so do we swimmers, and at this stage in my swimming career, I'm a forty-metre swimmer in a fifty-metre pool.

I stop, gasp for breath, just find my feet. I look rapidly around, as if this must be someone else's fault, and see a bloke being photographed by the side of the pool. In the last soft rays of the sun, he is absurdly beautiful. I flip up my goggles for a better look, and learn from the next day's *Manly Daily*, with the sun setting over the man's broad shoulders in the photograph, that he's the Australian short-course breaststroke champion. That automatically makes him a world contender, and yesterday we were swimmers in the same municipal Olympic pool which costs less than £2 for all-day entry.

It may not be like this everywhere in Australia, but it's like this here.

In Manly, there are any number of people who know what it takes. I wish the English were more certain about what that was, especially in an Ashes summer. We could then attend to whatever it was that had been going so wrong. What *does* it take? In a small population, the champions who know the secret formula inevitably live in the next house, or the next street; they went to the same school, they wear flip-flops to the beach like everyone else. Just ask someone who's been there, done that. They know what it takes, and they'll tell me what it is.

I meet Debbie Watson in a modish coffee shop just off the Corso, and underneath the table there's a long way between the middle of Debbie's fleece and the ends of her toes. She's dressed as a top-of-the-range PE teacher, white polo shirt with the collar up, navy-blue fleece. That's because, in a school up the road, she's a top-of-the-range PE teacher. Her hair, going grey at the sides, is tied back, and she has practical stud earrings and fit brown eyes, bright and clear. She's a fantastically capable-looking woman and an Olympic gold medallist and I'll flinch if she mentions a boyfriend.

Debbie was born up the hill in Manly Hospital in 1965, and she got off to a good sporting start. Like everyone else, she was surrounded as a child by top-class athletes.

'My dad played for Australia,' she tells me, stirring her coffee, smiling at the memory.

'What sport?'

'Every sport. That's what he told us. You name it, he'd done it.'

By the age of ten Debbie was a promising swimmer and netball player. 'I don't consider myself a massively competitive person,' she says, but by the age of fourteen she was having her first knee reconstruction. She had a second one a year later. That was the end of netball, and water sports it was from then on in. In 1993 she was voted the best water polo player in the world, and in 2000 she came out of retirement to inspire Australia to gold at the Sydney Olympics.

Water polo is a tough game, a fact revealed to the widest possible audience by the 1956 Olympics in Melbourne. The Hungary vs USSR semi-final was cut short due to blood-slicks in the pool. The Hungarians were in a sensational fury after the recent Soviet invasion of their country, a motivational technique no modern Olympic committee has yet tried to emulate. Imagine if you arranged an invasion, and then the invading country failed to make the play-off stages. What a waste of lottery money.

The main rivals to Australia during Debbie's career at the top were the USA, Canada, and more recently Hungary and Holland. Because I'm determined not to be inhibited by the Cringe, even in the presence of an

Australian Olympic gold medallist who's been through mysteries I can only dimly guess at, I ask about the rivalry with England, or Britain. Debbie laughs.

'You guys have a massive pool problem.'

She's right, we don't have the pools. More importantly, we don't have the showers. I love the showers at the Charlton pool, outside in the sunshine, with the shower head just below the top of a brick wall, above it only blue sky and some barbed wire to keep the screaming Manly girls out. The sun makes rainbows in the steam and I learn that however long I stay in there, a faint smell of chlorine lingers for the rest of the day. Across the table, Debbie is so fresh and clean I like to imagine this as something we have in common.

'Has England ever beaten Australia at women's water polo?' I ask.

Debbie looks perplexed.

'Has England ever *played* Australia?'

She thinks hard. She is a kind person, and she wants to be helpful. 'They must have a team,' she offers hopefully. 'Probably they do.'

Without more athletes like Debbie Watson, probably seems the best we can ever hope to manage. I submit to the Direct Cringe.

'Debbie, how can we be more like you? What do we have to do to be world-beaters?'

'The world?' Debbie laughs. 'First you have to beat the men.'

Daylight bathing in Manly immediately caused problems, and one of the most obvious problems was women. What should they wear? At first, this was also a problem for men, who were supposed to wear costumes from neck to knee, with skirts on top, as a double covering of the genital area. The pragmatic Aussies laughed this one off the beach by prancing about in their sisters' frocks, but the sisters weren't so lucky. Along with a ruined frock the bad news was that even by 1915 a woman's swimming costume in Australia was expected to be 'sportswoman-like . . . simple, tight, and short yet impenetrable'. This impenetrability is disturbing enough, without the *Sydney Morning Herald*'s added fabric suggestion that costumes should be made of 'scratchy wool', which 'defies the X-ray glance of the wowser'. It seems likely that thickness was more important than texture, except as a titillating detail for male daydreamers. Penetration *and* scratchy wool. Post-Victorian heaven.

It was at swimming that women first rivalled men in elite sport, and not just in Australia. Women were allowed to take swimming seriously because submerged, the body was mostly hidden. Men were spared the unsettling spectacle of female exertion and, as an added advantage, could ignore the possibility that women sometimes sweat.

Underwater, perspiration hidden, in 1926 US swimmer Gertrude Ederle swam the English Channel two hours faster than the previous best male time. This is one of the rare achievements that remains unassailable, because no Australian is ever going to match that, to Calais and back, not starting from New South Wales.

This meant that swimming was never entirely dominated by men, although the Australian swimming authorities did try to stop Fanny Durack, world record-holder in the 100 metres freestyle, and her close rival Mina Wylie, from travelling to the 1912 Stockholm Olympics. The justification they used was a brilliant piece

of sophistry, in the highest tradition of sports administrators everywhere. They found a rule stipulating that
women couldn't compete when men were present. The
Olympic selectors were men. How tragic. Although confident that Durack and Wylie were splendid competitors,
it was unfair to select them on reputation alone, and the
girls would have to stay at home. A popular campaign
unmasked this charade, and at Stockholm Durack and
Wylie duly won gold and silver for Australia.

They were welcomed back as champions, and attitudes
quickly changed. In Manly, women's sport started to
matter, and as early as 1925 the town council thought it
worth recording the name of a Miss E.W. Quirk, winner of
a competition for the Most Popular Manly Sporting Lady.
The fact that she was the mayor's daughter is surely
irrelevant. Debbie Watson was also honoured by the
Manly council, as Manly Citizen of the Year 2000. She
received a certificate, a glass bowl and the opportunity to
make a speech on Australia Day in praise of Australia. She
is not related to anyone currently in high office.

'The Olympics make a difference,' Debbie tells me, 'for
all of us, and for the simple reason that Australian women
are usually far more successful than the men. The rest of
the time progress is slower.'

She hunts through her bag for today's (Australian)
Telegraph, and brings it out slapping a front-page picture
of an aspiring ironwoman on the arm of a disgraced
Wallaby rugby player. 'What's she ever done? Or if she
has done something, she should be there in her own
right.'

Debbie takes a sadder example, of the international
rower turned cyclist who earlier that week had been run
down in Germany. A teenage driver had smashed into the

entire Australian women's cycling squad. A double international, Amy Gillett was also working for a doctorate.

'She was an amazing woman. She had to get killed to get in the paper.'

If women in Australia don't get the recognition they deserve, why do they carry on? Why did Debbie stick at it until the medal was around her neck? Why is she a winner?

'Plenty of people have the talent,' she says modestly, 'but not everyone can make the sacrifices. Studying especially, and a decent job.'

These sacrifices are more apparent when it's over. As a retired champion, Debbie seems, if not regretful, then wistful for that other life that might have been. There is a nagging doubt about whether it was worth it, a small drift of blue across the dazzle of seventeen years international sport to end up childless, unmarried, a PE teacher with an Olympic medal in a sock drawer. Debbie sometimes takes the medal out and looks at it, and moves it into her jumper drawer.

'I mean I learnt stuff,' she says. 'It made me a better person, but in a team way. I'm far more willing to fight for someone else than I am for myself.'

She confesses that swimming training is 'incredibly monotonous', but that may be a lesson in itself. 'Kids today are overstimulated. They have an unrealistic expectation of how much fun everything should be.' Only an elite athlete, a genuine achiever, can afford the insight that sport is worthwhile because it *isn't* fun. 'That's why, after the Olympics, I went cold turkey.'

Debbie decided to stop all competitive sport. It wasn't entirely a free choice. She couldn't run because of her knees, her bicep tore away from the tendon, and she had bone shaved off an injured shoulder, all injuries she'd played through on the way to the Olympic final.

'You must be glad to see the back of it.'

'Well, I'm training again with the Manly B squad at the Charlton pool. But otherwise I'm not competitive at all.'

'Me neither.'

'Apart from a few ocean races.'

'Nothing.'

'And I swam in the Australian corporate games.'

'Peanuts.'

'I play a bit of tennis, in a mixed doubles league. I can hit the ball quite hard.'

'Does mixed doubles count?'

'And I'm learning golf, but I don't like it much. I always feel afterwards like taking some proper exercise.'

I ask her if she owns a sofa.

'Yes, I do. I play games of cards on it with my boyfriend.' That's it. I flinch. My day is ruined.

'But I'm so not competitive.'

'I know so exactly what you mean.'

Whatever motivated Debbie to take on the world and win, it wasn't the money. After the Olympics, she received the government's A$15,000 gold-medal bounty, plus another A$5,000 from other corporate rewards. So that's A$20,000 for a seventeen-year career, in which the overseas expense allowance for the national women's water polo squad was twenty dollars per person per week. That's about eight pounds. A *week*.

'So why did you win?'

'The home Olympics was a huge advantage,' she says. At last, some good news for Britain. 'We had the attitude that we were battlers, and that we'd worked harder and trained harder and been less well rewarded than anyone else. We stayed in crappier accommodation and always, always, had to travel further to wherever the latest international tournament was happening.'

Someone tell the British Olympic Committee. Call off the US invasion. What's needed is not more money, but less, although following this argument the British should already be supreme across the world. In the cold north, on a training schedule of freezing mornings and rain-lashed roadwork, with added units of underfunding and a horrific diet, self-pity as a motivational tool should be our biggest single sporting asset.

In which case, we must be lacking something else, perhaps some essential unity of purpose. In a crunch situation, Debbie's Australian water polo team would gather at the side of the pool and say 'trenches'. It was a key word, and I ask her if they ever considered others: 'bayonets,' or 'gas'. Debbie won't be shaken by flippancy, and says the Anzac story is a rousing one.

'If the boys can do it, we can.'

Debbie Watson inspires me. I walk away from the café with her words slowly twisting in my mind: if the boys can do it, she can, if she can, I can. Following Debbie's example, I'm so not competitive that I go swimming at the Boy Charlton pool every day until I'm confident I can swim fifty metres of Australian crawl without sinking, whatever the conditions. I'm not ready to give up on beating the Australians, not yet. Time hasn't been called, and steaming in the outside rainbow showers at the pool, working on my writer's tan, a former non-swimmer, I find I still believe I can do anything if I put my mind to it. Maybe by now I'd be a triathlon champion, if only I'd left the shallow end at the Milton Road Baths.

There's only one way to find out, and the next Sunday morning early at eight I'm catching a bus with Bobby Yonks. We're on our way to Curl Curl Beach for the weekly swim meet of the Frigid Frogs.

'Croak! Croak!'

The Frogs' war cry brings the club to order on the open veranda of their clubhouse. It overlooks the long yellow beach curling away for more than a kilometre to the next headland. Immediately below us is the ocean pool, a green chunk of ocean restrained as a rectangle. The long sides measure fifty metres, and men are sea-fishing off the flat whitewashed restraining wall. There are some bent and rusting fence-poles as a further token boundary against the Pacific, but the waves break and race along the wall-tops, filling the pool, overflowing it, then receding. The fishermen in rubber boots shuffle away as above the clubhouse the Frogs raise their flag, green and white against the blue sky, with a fat red frog in the middle.

Today, there's a visit from another winter swimming club, the North Curl Curl Cool Cats, who use the ocean pool at the other end of the beach. This is not an ambitious away trip, but it merits a barbecue and two kegs of beer, the set menu of old Australians at play. By old, I mean unreconstructed, pre-multicultural, with bursting red faces and moustaches and huge uncovered bellies, usually with something to say about why the Frigid Frogs is better without women involved.

'It's just mates, mate.'

Old Australia has often been criticised for being a monoculture of beer and sport. But that's two cultures already, and it also has its own language. In any dialogue that follows, insert 'mate' or 'fuck' with abandon. Those two words are as sure as the sunshine, as regular as punctuation, though the Frogs may not know it was women who originally claimed the fuck patois for Australia. Convict maids used to swear freely at their prim mistresses, knowing the fine ladies could rarely bring themselves to repeat the words to a judge or a husband.

'Yes, my darling, she called me a . . .'

'A what, sweet pea?'

'A f . . . f . . . f . . .'

'A free settler, my loved one?'

'A c . . . c . . . c . . .'

'A kindly mistress?'

'Nothing, my chuckle-bun. Never mind.'

A huge, flat-faced man shouts in my direction, without moving from his bar stool, which is out on its own in the middle of the veranda: 'So you're the Pommy cunt.' Ah, this must be the famous Pom-bashing. He shouts again, looking around for support: 'Don't know too many Pommies.'

I take off my sunglasses, like the army officer in the recruitment ad – it's supposed to reduce the kind of tension that leads to outbreaks of physical violence. You can learn a lot from TV adverts, or from the British army, but the training's easier for watching TV.

'I know a Pommy,' says someone else, and I brace myself for a bruising punchline. It comes defiantly. 'My father.'

Bobby Yonks takes me aside and apologises in his generous, halting manner, muttering about education and upbringing. I know he doesn't believe what he's saying, but he's making allowances on my behalf, an effort to see things from the other side. 'Ignore it,' he says unconvincingly. 'It doesn't mean anything.'

I'm introduced as a 'visitor from the old country'. This

is ironic, surely, or a habit of speech. Inevitably, after making the circuit, I find myself in front of the huge man on the stool. He is now without his shirt, and he's introduced to me as the Whale. He is vast, a non-swimming member beached and wallowing on his bar stool with a plastic cup of beer smothered in bloated fingers. The pocked blubber from his white belly trembles and rolls over his hips, a folding barrel of herrings rounding out and flattening over his thighs, sweat and gallons of Cretaceous oil seeping from the crease of each sea-mammal fold.

'So,' I say, just another Pommy cunt making chit-chat, 'Why do they call you the Whale?'

Only two members have ever been expelled from the Frigid Frogs: one of them 'because he was fucking swearing all the time' and the other 'because he was an arsehole'. All these men seem huge to me, a mixture of meat and beer and hard muscle gone to seed. There is an unmistakable sense of territoriality and vague threat. I also know there's a deal on offer. If I can be called Pommy cunt a significant number of times, and not hit anyone, or collapse in tears (*England Collapse*), some essential territorial point will have been made. I will have rolled over, and we can be chums.

'Pommy cunt! Want a beer?'

If I don't like it, it means I can't take a joke, I'm 'up myself', but nothing is entirely funny, especially here. The platypus, apparently the most comic of Australian beasts, has a poisonous spur on its back legs.

I seek out the Frigid Frogs handicapper (another official-looking table, more ledgers) to get my placing for the heats, and because I'm honest (it takes me about seventy seconds to swim fifty metres) I get called in the first heat, first lane, reserved for the day's worst swimmer. Or for Pommy cunts. However, I've learnt about handicapping and deceit from the hypocrisy of golf, and if I win, even off a handicap, I'm still the winner.

I get called off the blocks, and the water is freezing, colder than the ocean, and I shriek down lane one of the ocean pool like a frozen cat. I make it to the end in fifty-six seconds. And have some puff left. I have obliterated the weakest and oldest swimmers in the Frigid Frogs, and the fact that I started in front of them is all part of life's rich handicap system. This is a triumph. Take that!

As a visitor, they won't let me swim in the final even though I won my heat, and I snaffle this as a compliment. Australians losing, running scared, exactly what I came to Australia to see. All smug and done, I can now relax and watch nearly naked Frogs in the more expert heats. Sport allows men to stare, in detail, without homosexuality alleged or feared. Especially in swimming, where in this all-male club bodies are straining, on their fronts, buttocks up, naked except for tiny Lycra Speedos. It's surely nothing but coincidence that everyone's favourite words are mate and fuck.

After the races the Frogs call the meeting to order – 'Croak! Croak!' – and everyone empties their loose change into a metal hospital bedpan for sins such as wearing a green shirt, or failing to fly in on a helicopter. Like school-boys, the Frogs exclude whatever life they have at home by using nicknames, passwords known only to initiates – Munz, the Whale, Fur Coat. There's Friendly, short for the Friendly Fed, a policeman who in forty years of service never made an arrest, suggesting exceptional arbitration skills or endemic corruption. I have no idea which, and no great desire to know. This is the Great Escape, not just

115

from women and home but from identities and respon-
sibilities and adulthood, only it's not so much an escape
as a poorly camouflaged hiding place. It's fat men behind
a thin tree.

Manly and primitive is not an attractive combination.
As the second keg is tapped, there's a slightly desperate,
end-of-term sense that the Frogs are enjoying each other's
company, in this place and in this way, while they still
can. The Bondi Icebergs, an equivalent winter swimming
club, now accept women members, but not the Frogs. Not
yet. The clubhouse, however, is council owned.

'All it takes is one busybody to ruin everything,' says
Stuart Gain, 'one woman on the council who calls what
we do discrimination and we're out.'

Stuart is a former bank manager and a Frigid Frog for
twenty-five years. I like talking to him, partly because he's
used to making conversation with ill-at-ease chancers, but
also because fuck mate beer Pommy cunt quickly gets
tedious. Stuart is a neat sixty-three with a well-trimmed
moustache and cheeky blue eyes – in the summer he
swims a kilometre every morning seven days a week. He
obviously loves the Frogs.

'This is where you learn who's a crook and who's good,'
he says proudly, so I look around and ask him who's a
crook.

'Well, not exactly criminal,' he corrects himself, 'some
of them dip onto the other side.'

'Am I a con man?'

'No,' he says, 'too relaxed. Or you're a bloody good one.'

I ask Stuart what makes the Australian male competitive, and he says the Irish blood. While it's true that
the Frogs clubhouse is boozy with O'Bruces, even as
nostalgia this particular theory has had its day. The Celt

in the Anglo-Celtic Australian is diluting as surely as the Anglo, and has been since the end of the White Australia policy, when Australia would take every immigrant under the age of forty-five, in good health, and white. In those days the immigration officers would take one look and decide entry with the infamous Dictation Test, which required any optimistic but suspiciously dark-skinned arrival to complete 200 words of dictation. In a language selected by the Australian officials.

The test was quietly withdrawn with the end of the Immigration Restriction Act in 1958. There was no referendum on the issue, or great public debate, and this may help explain the brief popularity of Pauline Hanson's right-wing One Nation party, and also those Frigid Frogs who now join us and mutter darkly about Greeks and Italians. It turns out that the children of the wogs, and they admit this, are now 'the finest people in the land'.

'There's something different, spiritual about this country,' Stuart says. 'It gets to you, so you feel attached to it. It worked on all the others, so it'll work on these Arab bastards.'

'You have faith in the land?'

'I do.'

Here in the unfurnished heart of anti-domestic masculinism, where women aren't permitted to make a difference, Stuart's concept of the seductive land is at least a consoling thought. I remember the strange self-contained strength of the National Park, and I'd like to pursue this idea, but Stuart keeps refusing more beer and glancing nervously out at the road.

'Fuck, mate,' Stuart says. 'Gotta be careful. The wife's coming to pick me up.'

* * *

Of the one and a half million British emigrants who arrived in Australia after the war, a quarter returned home, most of them to England. An official Australian report from 1967 was in no doubt why. The returnees 'lacked character'.

Unofficially, they were Whingeing Poms.

The Whingeing Pom is an invention of the post-war period, because up until 1945, the whingeing was seen as being about equal. When the first transport ships slipped down the Thames, the English middle classes whinged that Australia wasn't a severe enough punishment, despite the fact that Sydney was not a great place for a holiday in 1788. The principal English whinge was that convicts would have been better engaged in chain gangs on public works, like they were in France. The first Australians may well have agreed, because they were starving. Even after they discovered Jackson Bay frothing with red snapper, they whinged that they preferred the old country's maggoty salt beef. Since then, historically, both sides have liked to whinge that the other is the bigger whinger. Pointing out a whinger is in itself a whinge, as is whingeing about being the whinger pointed out.

Whingeing has become a normative, even repressive, Australian scold, and can describe behaviour any individual Australian happens not to like, from romantic melancholy to a fear of poisonous insects to not drinking a second gallon of Carlton Draught before vomiting in the doorway of a kebab shop. These days no one is safe, but whingeing started out as any complaint about a minor inconvenience that ultimately makes no difference. The fairness of the accusation then depends on what counts as minor.

For the post-war Poms, the loudest complaint was

against the conditions in migrant hostels. Families arriving from England were issued with knife, fork, spoon, toilet roll, and then shown the toilet facilities, usually fly-infested outdoor blocks with canvas doors. Families of five were billeted in tightly subdivided cubicles in woolsheds, or given two rooms in half a Nissen hut, a semi-cylindrical bend of corrugated iron that in the summer had to be hosed down to stop it acting like an oven on the babies sleeping inside. High rents made it difficult for immigrant families to move into independent housing, and after a hard day's work Mum and Dad came home to kids with questions from their new Australian school: 'Mum, what's a Pommy bastard?'

Perhaps such challenges were minor, even though James Jupp, Australia's foremost researcher into immigration, calls these government-run hostels 'a fraud and a disgrace'. But levels of comfort are relative: in 1971 an Australian water company reported that 75 per cent of Manly residents said they didn't mind swimming in raw sewage. Didn't want to whinge.

In a sense, every British immigrant was born a whinger. Voting with the feet was a type of complaint, an alertness to something wrong or unsatisfactory at home. The true non-whingeing stoics stayed in England and played *Barrier Reef* in the garden, nurturing the Recreational Cringe. (To play *Barrier Reef* in the early 1970s in Swindon, you needed a sunny day in the long summer holidays and a blue plastic paddling pool. Shuffle into the garden fully equipped for deep-sea diving, with mask, snorkel and flippers falsely extorted by lying about proficiency in swimming. Sit on the edge of the pool facing outwards away from the water, feet on the grass. Then kick off and topple in backwards. This was utterly un-Australian and completely safe, seeing as the water was shark-free and twenty inches deep.)

The post-war British immigrants couldn't understand why Australians weren't better pleased to see them. They were British, *English*, from the tried old stock that had discovered Australia in the first place. The Australians should have welcomed them, been grateful that someone had bothered to make the effort.

What? *What?* Whingers *and* arrogant? Bloody Poms.

One of the more dependable aspects of our famous English arrogance is the assumption that no genuine ill will exists between us and our former English-speaking colonies. Let's start with the Ashes. The original obituary for English cricket, published in 1882 by the *Sporting Times*, clearly states that 'The Body will be cremated and the ashes taken to Australia.' This is not what happened. The four-inch urn has left London only twice, briefly in 1988 for Australia's Bicentennial celebrations and then again at the end of 2006. The rest of the time it's kept jealously in the MCC Cricket Museum at Lord's, a fixed exhibit of the kind of English duplicity Australians have learned to recognise.

In the Australian Book of Life, the British drop them in it. Only native Australian resourcefulness can get them back out again. This is a relationship patterned and then stitched through the history of the twentieth century. After the shambles of Gallipoli, the British were so appreciative of the Anzac sacrifice that we asked them to pay for it. The Australian government was billed for every penny spent on Australian troops during the course of the First World War. The economic depression in Australia in the 1930s, which saw families living on beaches in shelters made of sacks and flattened oil tins, was accelerated by English banks draining the economy with untimely demands for debt repayment. In World War II Roosevelt and Churchill put their heads together, compared tobaccos and hats, then decided the Japanese could do what they liked with Australia. At least until the war was over in Europe.

The British even managed to blame the bungled defence of Singapore on Australian cowardice, compiling a War Office report of unfavourable eye-witness impressions: 'They [Anzacs] were soon lying all over the streets of Singapore dead drunk,' said one British observer. 'I have never seen men such absolute cowards and so thoroughly frightened. What fine soldiers. If America wants Australia, let her have it and good riddance to a damn rotten crowd.' This from the familiar supply of British attitudes that included the secretary of the golf club refusing to allow defensive gun emplacements on his precious golf course. Not until he'd consulted the committee.

Between 1952 and 1963, when many British citizens were considering emigration as a viable escape from the pathology of nuclear Europe, the British government carried out A-bomb tests at Emu Field and Maralinga in central Australia. These explosions contaminated 'extensive areas' of the outback, and mean that Australia remains, with Japan, one of only two industrialised countries to have nuclear bombs dropped on it by a foreign power. Just in case Australians hadn't got the message, the 1971 UK Immigration Act ended their special privilege of 'free and full right of entry' into Britain. In 1994 travel restrictions were further tightened.

Against this background, sporting victories could seem immensely important, an indirect yet aggressive resistance as the Cultural Cringe was turned inside out. It wasn't a convict heritage that made the sporting rivalry matter to Australians, but repeated, up-to-the-minute abuses and the energy of every new wave of immigrants. Australia took more immigrants from Britain than anywhere else every year from 1945 until 1996, so no wonder the fixture had vim, especially as most Brits who came to Australia and stayed were the up and at 'em type. Had to be.

In the nineteenth century, even free settlers to Australia were thought to be inferior to stay-at-home yeomen, because adventurers evidently lacked stability, and steadiness. There was a sense they hadn't been able to hack it at home, weaklings forced from the tribe. In my lifetime, initiative and enterprise have been more highly valued than steadiness. It makes for a better film of the book of the life. There's an old convict joke that Australia was destined for greatness because its people were chosen by the finest judges in England. In fact, they had and still have our best people, self-selecting, brave enough to live in the cinematic present, excelling at the here and now.

Which is always going to be useful at 78 for 3 on a seaming wicket. Australians, whether the family arrived in 1805 or 1974, can relax and play their shots because in their recent history, whenever they were very unhappy, they moved along. In the future, or even some time soon, if they're very unhappy they can move along again. Don't Sweat the Small Stuff. For Men. We just stayed, accepting grey days and melancholy as inescapable horrors of existence, and wrote poetry about it. What a bunch of whingers.

Beaches exist as a cure for whingeing. With a hangover from the Frigid Frogs, Monday morning feels like that downtime of the tour when an England cricketer needs to unwind with a spliff or break a bed with a barmaid. Despite my surprise victory in the pool, horror flashbacks from the first tee at Manly golf course have me whimpering at unexpected moments. I find this morning I'm in repressible form, a repressible character, while hoping my daily visit to the beach will turn things round.

The beach is more resonant of modern Australia than that other frontier, the bush. As Lawrence wrote in *Kangaroo*, 'Go into the middle of Australia and see how empty it is. You can't face emptiness long. You have to come back and do something to keep from being frightened at your own emptiness, and everything else's emptiness.' The thought of all that outback drove Australians to distraction, to the games fields and new ways of keeping themselves occupied on the broad Pacific beaches. The beach became a distinct arena for self-definition and testing, 'making our young men manly and hardy'. Maybe the beach is the secret to Australian success.

Manly's ocean beach preserves the slightly detached, wistful feel of a holiday resort receding from its heyday, in Manly's case the 1940s. It is both itself and the idealised place its visitors would like it to be, as if those of us here on a sunny winter's day aren't living our lives but our memories. It's second nature for families to pose their day at Manly beach like a photograph, and in every couple, or so it seems, the girl in a bikini is with her favourite boyfriend before her husband.

These happy snapshots can be misleading. The first recorded accident in Manly, apart from Governor Phillip's spearing, was a drowning. In July 1816, the two sons of stockman John Randall were lost at an unspecified point off the Manly coastline. There was another double drowning in 1902, when Frederick Smalpage tried to save a Manly chambermaid, Mabel Thorp. At that time, safety equipment consisted of a basic lifeline on the beach, attached to a buoy, and some local men grabbed the buoy and swam out to help Smalpage who was helping Thorp. The lifeline broke, and the men had trouble swimming back in again. Someone grabbed the spare. It too broke, and by then there was no one left to save. Smalpage's body was later recovered. Of Mabel Thorp nothing remained, except, turning slowly on the surface of the water, her straw holiday hat.

The hat is important. It suggests that Mabel Thorp was not a sporting swimmer. She may even have been a paddler, surprised by a stronger wave, and it was this preventable drowning that led to the foundation of the Life Saving Club at Manly. Not that everyone thought lifesavers were necessary.

Manly has a history of mayors loyal to a fault. In 1906 Mayor Quirk, father of the 1924 Most Sporting Manly Lady, challenged the number of drownings reported at Manly. These deaths were no accidents, he claimed indignantly, every single one of them was a suicide. As such, Manly's record on beach safety remained irreproachable. James Bonner, Quirk's successor, took a similar approach to Manly's nine cases of bubonic plague. Surely not, he said, there was only the one, and that was 'from outside'.

In Britain, most electors would recognise this bluster as self-serving political expediency. In Australia it's simply being chipper, staying faithful to the national preoccupation with avoiding any hint of a whinge. This means that in Australian politics, as in Australian life, the facts will always be worse than anyone cares to admit.

This is very useful in the plotting of soap operas, because despite their reputation for straight talking, a spade to an Australian is rarely known as a spade. It's a provisional measure before trading up to a mechanical digger. In the meantime, diggers, get on with the digging.

So however idyllic the beach seems, it is in fact a bitterly contested space. The present mayor, Dr Peter Macdonald, has various Manly problems to keep him busy – an ageing population, rising house prices, his attempt to limit late-night violence by cutting licensing hours, and letters in the paper blasting Manly Corso as the 'sewer of the Northern Beaches'.

He also has the never-say-die attitude of his sporting constituents. They've got football and volleyball and rugby and Australian Rules and bowls and golf and croquet and shooting and ocean pools and a beach. But when I ask around for questions to put to the mayor they say – 'Ronald McDonald? Yeah, why haven't we got an AstroTurf? Why haven't we got an *ice rink*?'

The mayor is wearing pressed beige trousers and a blue shirt with a tartan tie, Australianised in sunshine yellow and orange. This is because he was once a Scot, though now reformed: fit, tanned, his white hair well cropped, a wearer of frameless glasses to expose the honesty of his public official's face. He's confident. He's backing himself.

'In twelve years on the council,' Macdonald says, Scottish accent largely intact, 'I can't remember a single complaint about too much money being spent on sport and recreation.'

I then get to see many pages of budget, but don't understand them.

'A politician can't ignore sport,' Macdonald tells me. He

interlaces his fingers and leans forward sincerely across the desk, 'Though it's sometimes hard to engage all the participants in rational debate. The surf club, for example. If I disagree with their point of view then I'm in favour of leaving children in the sea to drown.'

'Are you?'

'Sport is a vote winner,' he adds crisply, 'in the sense that the community values sport. As do I.'

Hardly surprising, as Mayor Macdonald of Manly was once a Scotland schoolboy rugby international, then an RAF doctor who went on a Combined Services Tour to the Far East in 1968, flew on to Australia and never looked back. Sport gave him travel and the confidence to cross the world aged twenty-nine with a young family on the Assisted Package Scheme.

'I have a fundamental belief that sport breeds basic principles in people,' he says. He acts on it, too – he is a member of the golf club and a jogger, ten to fifteen kilometres every other day because physically fit is mentally fit – and I believe him not because he's a politician but a doctor. Sport is good for health, for discipline and self-esteem and social skills and much more besides. It's also useful training for the strategies, conflicts and infringements endemic in local politics.

Poor Dr Macdonald. He authorised the five beach volley-ball courts lined up on the sand close to the promenade wall opposite the Manly Pacific Hotel. They don't look much: two square wooden posts and a head-high net. However, they're permanent structures occasionally used for private profit, so the council receives complaints about encroachment on the basic Australian principle of open public access to the beach. Manly Surf School is criticised for the same reason. The fact that Manly is the home of beach volleyball, now an Olympic sport, is irrelevant in the context of this particular hundred years' war.

Manly people have been protective of their public space since as long ago as 1903, when the Life Saving Club began a ten-year petition for a clubhouse at South Steyne overlooking the beach. This seemed to make sense, from a lifesaving point of view, and a century and three buildings later, the Manly Life Saving Club is a flat-roofed concrete structure with a large second floor balcony and sundeck. Overlooking the beach. The club has 1,500 members and one part-time paid secretary, who is ill. This means that Ben Wotton, a lifesaver since 1971 at the age of fourteen, Vice-president, Sponsorship Committee Member, Public Officer, Tour Manager, Financial Trustee and Beach Sprint Captain, is dealing with the admin backlog in a tiny office on the second floor.

The door is open, and probably always open, because a photocopied sheet is taped where everyone can see it:

<u>Vale</u>
Malcolm 'Bagpipes' MacDonald
Long Serving Member
Passed Away
16 July after a long
illness.
A good bloke who will
Be missed.

And inside, the office is cramped by a photocopier and shelves of box files, a water pistol, an Australian Rules footie, a rugby ball and a pair of yellow waterproof binoculars. There's a Tupperware lost property box containing piles of keys and a tennis ball.

Ben, 6 foot 6, black-haired, healthy, is wearing shorts and a T-shirt. He tells me the club is like a great big family.

'Right,' I say.

'Yeah,' he adds. 'Mate. But not the von Trapps coming singing over the mountain.'

Australia's lifeguards were once inseparable from the British idea of Australia, a regular feature in *Look and Learn*. Lifesavers were the lords of the ocean beaches, icons of masculinity, as made-in-Australia as the Sydney Harbour Bridge. They were hard-bodied models of discipline and humanitarianism, in one-piece bathing suits and snappily-strapped swimming caps, but I can't remember the last time I saw them celebrated. Yes, I can. At the Sydney Olympics they appeared, finally, right at the end of the closing ceremony, in a kind of ironic *mise en scène* with Kylie Minogue. I didn't get it myself. Was someone trying to suggest that lifesavers were gay?

Ben doesn't think so, though gay lifesavers are as welcome in the Manly Life Saving Club as anyone else. Times change, and quickly. It was only in 1981 that women could join the surf lifesaving movement, which partly explains why *Baywatch* was set in America. It's also because the first Australian women lifesavers were sometimes known as Pogs. This was not a term of endearment, and Pamela Anderson wouldn't have stood for it. It was a combination of pig and dog, as if the square-headed clubbies at that time couldn't quite decide, or spell. Now, 30 per cent of Manly lifesavers are women, and this year women members won club person of the year in all three age categories.

I ask Ben about the British.

'Of all the visitors,' he says, 'they're the best. They show the lifesavers respect.'

Of course they do. The mums and dads had *Look and Learn*.

'The British hooligans are at Bondi, of course.'

A lot of British migrants join up. It's a conspicuous way of becoming Australian, and a fantasy I share for many seconds until Ben describes the requirements for the bronze medallion. This is the minimum qualification needed to strap on the yellow and red hat, and it involves swimming 400 metres in under nine minutes (in a pool or the ocean – I decide!).

A burnished and portly older man shuffles into the office. He is naked apart from some curly white chest-hair and dark trunks. It's not for me to say, as far as trunks go, how small is too small, but in Manly this type of trunk is called the budgie-smuggler. He's just out of the water and he drips on the mail and the latest sponsor printouts.

'We still get called clubbie dickheads,' Ben says, 'sometimes.' He shakes water off a letter from the bank. 'But people have children and then their perceptions change.'

If Ben is one side of a contest for the beach, Mike 'Froth' Taylor is the other. In the 1960s and '70s it was clubbies against surfies, the Australian equivalent of mods against rockers, and surfers vied with lifesavers to be lords of the Australian beach – who now was the winner?

I trudge back along the sand to North Steyne, and catch Mike between lessons, sitting on a plastic chair outside the surf hut. He plants an extra chair and we look at the waves like grounded sea captains. Or not quite: Mike is wearing square dark glasses and a green baseball hat with *Hawaii* on it. His blond curls bubble out the back. He has a sun-faded yellow *Manly Surf School* T-shirt and knee-length denim shorts. A silver watch and a thumb ring. Like in California, a fantastic smile compensates for a chronic shades habit. Eyes hidden, the expression is all in the mouth, the white teeth, and in Mike's case, a dashing silver tongue stud (you can get them in the tattoo parlour by the library – 'One small prick for a lifelong stud', or so says the sign in the window).

'What's so good about surfing, Mike?'

He surveys the waves, thinking hard about my question, sometimes tonguing his upper lip, the stud glinting in the sunlight.

'Rich,' he says, turning to me decisively, 'what *isn't* good about it?'

'What about the clubbies?'

'That's different,' Mike says. 'They see the surf as an obstacle course. They race through it, and then race straight back. They make everything a competition. What's the fun in that?'

I walk back down the beach, scuffing the sand between my toes.

'Ben,' I say, 'what's the fun in that?'

'In what, Rich?'

'In making everything a competition.'

For Ben Wotton, born and bred in Manly, it's in the blood. His dad was a track athlete, for several years the Australian 400 metres hurdles champion. Naturally. Ben's event was soft-sand sprinting, reaching twelve Australian finals, and his eyes light up as he talks about the summer surf carnivals, the great sports fests of the lifesaver clubs. To compete, and this includes televised professional Ironman races, every competitor must be a serving member of a lifesaving club, and up to date with their volunteer patrols.

They can then join in with competitive beach sprints, surf-skiing, board-riding, ski-paddling, flag races, swimming. They even have competitive first aid (Manly won gold at the nationals). Remember Mabel Thorp. Sport in Australia saves lives, and none of these events is contested in a holiday straw hat. My own personal favourite, to watch, is the surfboats, rowed by four lifesavers with heavy oars and a standing sweep in the back. When the boat turns to catch the surf, silhouetted along the blazing highway of sun on the ocean, the rowers look like the first sailors coming ashore, an endless re-enactment of conquest.

'The sport's just a glue,' Ben says, his excitement subsiding as he pushes his glasses back up his nose. 'The club is primarily a rescue service, though the idea is we don't actually want to rescue people. It's less unfun to drag someone out of the water while they're still breathing.'

'See?' Mike says, when I make it back to his little square of the beach. 'For them, it's either an obstacle or a danger. Now to surfers, the surf is . . .'

'What is it, Mike?'

'It's . . . like . . . er . . .' And Mike is waiting for a wave here, of inspiration. He leans forward with his elbows on his knees, the truth position, hands together in prayer, fingers pointing at the ocean. He nods his head approvingly at a slow-breaking left to righter. 'It's a spiralling path . . . a pleasure . . . um . . . a chute . . . like flying a . . . vehicle . . . it's a ride . . .' he laughs, 'man, if you get it, it's a Hallmark card.'

'A what?'

'A Hallmark card, mate. It's your birthday, Christmas, everything.'

I'm not impressed. Is that it? Is that *all*?

Surfers used to 'dance with Krishna' – they were edge-riders on waves synonymous with God, and other such hazy flimflam arriving from California in the '60s. But at least it had ambition – surfing was a path to enlightenment, which made older Australians nervous. Early attempts to stifle this off-the-wallness included the obligatory registration of surfboards and compulsory third-party insurance. Measures that had tamed commuters didn't work on surfers, but crazy-paved philosophy and dope were ultimately no match for the Australian way of life. In a story of the Australian way meets the American way, the Australians stayed in character and won.

They made surfing competitive.

In May 1964 the first official world surfing championship was held at Manly Beach. Its sponsors were Ampol petrol, Trans Australian Airways and Manly council. Groovy, it was not. In front of a 65,000 crowd, the championship of the world was won by local Manly boy Bernard 'Midget' Farrelly, who was not actually a midget, because that would be too good to be true.

Australian culture could now adopt surfing as a sport, a term that implied structure and discipline, and the Australians went on to develop an entirely new surf style based on athleticism and aggression. It was pioneered by Aussie surfer Nat Young, who skipped the audition for Krishna's dance partner and 'ripped the shit out of the waves'. Nice one, mate. The ocean became another rival to overcome, and this style is now the international normative standard. Any day on Manly Beach you can see young gun contenders hopping and bouncing their boards on fading waves, a sign of petulance towards the Pacific, of disappointment, as if to say, 'Is that all you've got?'

This attitude hasn't always made Australian surfers popular. Imagine the Chappell brothers on holiday and it's easy to understand why, in the winter of 1976–7, the surf shops of Hawaii refused to supply boards to any Australians at all until they could 'learn to be humble'. The locals also threatened to burn down houses where Australians were staying, so Jeff Thomson must have been there too.

Having said that, Australian-style attitude is also what made surfing a global marketing miracle. A boy, sunglasses, bleached blond dreadlocks, walks along the beach wearing a T-shirt saying *Ocean and Earth: Surfing is my Religion*. Surfing's free and easiness had a remarkably brief life, and is now just the silver lining on the image that surf entrepreneurs steal, distort, repackage and sell back to the kids, with the added edge of ripping the shit from the ocean. In that context, *Pray for Surf* reads better than *Pray for Profit*, and the money floods in from landlocked towns in cold countries, every concrete skate park a breaking Manly wave.

Mike isn't immune. He has a moneymaking idea and has applied for a patent he won't talk about. He's right not to talk about it because otherwise I'd have said what it was, but it's to do with surfing. It's a storage solution. And the solution is: buy a VW camper van and put the board on the roof. Storage problem solved. Not that I blame Mike. I hope he gets rich from his patent because I never understood the problem of killing the goose that lays the golden eggs. Nothing lives for ever, not even the fashion for surfing, so the goose was going to die in any case.

When he makes it as the richest surfer in Manly, Mike is going to buy a house with a yard. And a dog. This is all that's left of soul-surfing, of the spiritual pursuit of the perfect wave.

But no! A regular sight on the beach is a tight huddle of five or six surfers in wetsuits. I've often wondered what they're doing, so today I stand close by, pretending to read the waves. They're *praying*. These surfers are huddled in prayer before running into the water because surfing is not their religion. They are the Christian Surfers, and they have to talk to me because it's in the Christian rules. Their chief, Nic Gilmour, is thirty-one years old and God has given him a fantastic set of teeth. He has a brown crew cut and round, wide-open, clear-blue eyes. And a brilliant smile.

'Surfing, mate? I'll tell you what it is. It's an experience with a lot of the other crap peeled off it.'

Nic is a full-time Christian Surfer and lives off 'faith support'. He just waits for God to deliver money, and God makes the deliveries. This is much closer to the mad, marginal life on the edge that surfing once aspired to being. If displaying irreverence towards cultural norms was the essence of original surf culture, then the Manly Christian Surfers are more genuinely living the difference than the drones in Quiksilver shorts watching Billabong ads on VH1.

'I look up into a steaming eight-foot barrel,' the grinning, gleaming Nic says, 'and I feel the divine hand.'

He has psalm 93:4 written on his board. 'The Lord on high is mightier than the noise of many waters, yea, than the mighty waves of the sea.' This is more like it, and even though Nic looks impatient to get out there, the Christian Surfers rise above impatience, just as I'd hoped to do when I first came to the beach to forget my humiliation at golf.

'You should come to the Jesus Pro-am,' Nic says, sensing my vulnerability, my Englishness. He knows that standing on a surfboard, I skitter like a lost sheep. 'Best event on the circuit.'

'Er. Is it religious?'

'Well,' Nic says, twinkling all over with seawater and salt distillations, the sun making a halo behind his head, 'if you come to a CS event, you're going to hear about Jesus.'

'Sorry, Nic. I meant to say, is it competitive?'

'Sure. Pro surfers need to feel the love as urgently as anyone else.'

Slightly disappointed, I walk up and down the beach, between the surfies and the clubbies and back again, and every time I pass the Christian Surfers I remember the beach is a contested space, the site for one competition after another.

Among surfers there are longboarders versus short-boarders versus bodyboarders, or 'lid-riders'. It was Nat Young who first disapproved of the bodyboard because 'you're on your stomach, you're a beaten man'. For lifesavers, at the other end of the beach, there's constant friction with professional council lifeguards, though the details of this competition may seem trivial when you lose consciousness and start floating face-down towards New Zealand.

'And Brazilians,' Mike adds, when I press him for anyone else he finds annoying. 'They get out there and they're a Harry. They're up themselves. They just don't get it.'

I goad Mike 'Froth' Taylor, the most positive human being on planet Manly. I want him to continue admitting it's not all good, as if this counts as a rare decisive victory over an Australian. 'Come on, Mike, apart from the clubbies and the Brazilians, what *else* gets you down?'

'The parking. And in the summer the people, but then if there weren't the people there wouldn't be Manly. My girlfriend, sometimes . . . No, that's good, it's all good, mate.'

'Come on, Mikey. What's bad about Manly beach?'

'The English! Ha!'

'Something else.'

'Mate, if you really want to know. It's the sun.'

At last, something Mike and Ben can agree on. It's the cancer, the premature ageing, and everyone in Australia now knows to slip slap slop. Or just stay indoors. Back at the surf club, Ben Wotton takes me out onto the second-floor deck and we look over the golden beach and the calming evening ocean. For a while we just look at it, because Mike and the Christian Surfers and bodyboarders and the council lifeguard and Mayor Macdonald and Manly Life Saving Club all have a less parochial worry than Aussies versus Poms. On a medium projection of the global greenhouse effect, the Pacific is predicted to rise twenty to thirty centimetres in the next thirty years.

'At high tide,' Ben tells me, nodding his head at everything we can see in front of us, 'that means no Manly Beach.'

'Jeepers. You're not just whingeing, are you, Ben?'

'Hey, mate,' Ben counters, turning his back on the ocean and the reflected sunset, thinking about getting back to his paperwork, 'it's an interesting challenge, not a show-stopper.'

So there it is. Australia versus global warming, and while the Australians respect their opponent, and wouldn't want to appear overconfident, they're backing themselves for a win. Sand can be shifted, levels raised. What a contest! Manly people against climate change and the habits of the planet, so that along with volleyball and surf sports Manly Beach surely now becomes, true to a claim made in the Life Saving Club 2005 Annual Report, 'one of the world's greatest sporting venues'.

Fourth Test

I would sooner die than be beaten, I hate the person that's beaten me and I hate myself worse for being beaten, and the young get that from me.

Percy Cerutty, ABC radio archive, 1970

Running is the humblest of recreational sports. Buy some shoes and shorts, start and finish at your own front door, and when you do get back you can trust the showers and don't have to wash with naked strangers. Unless you're a student, in which case your life has many other compensations as well as this one.

For that Hallmark card feeling, that stand-up cardboard reminder of Happy Birthday, Getting Married, Your First Child feeling, I can try running. It's easier than surfing, and I don't have to be tenacious and talented like Debbie Watson – run often and far enough and I too can have a full knee reconstruction. Nor do I have to start aged fourteen, take lessons, or pass a safety test. I can just get out there in the Australian sunshine and run.

In the *Manly Daily*, the paper I read every day, there's a letter from Mr Golding, 52, who believes 'you can get past the most incredible things by believing in yourself and being persistent'. This is today's familiar Hollywood narrative, the liveable dream, the orthodox belief of our times. You can make it if you want to, if you want to enough.

Running is a training drill for this popular story, an exercise in self-believing and persistence. Put one foot in front of the other, but a little faster than that, and from now on running isn't about skill but about will.

I've always liked running, and more so as I get older, as if I'm keen to use up my body before I die. Wouldn't want to waste it. I'm also getting close to the age where many men decide they need to run a marathon. There's no clearer cry for help from the onset of a midlife crisis – one last crippling hurrah. The light is dying, and months of pounding and sweating might reverse the decision, might delay the dimmer switch on the dying of the light.

Fringe benefits include getting out of the house and then, unlike other sports, avoiding meaningful human contact. It's a brief inner trip to the wilderness, and it's surprising that Patrick White, novelist of the great Australian interior, couldn't understand this. He was no great fan of sport, believing his fellow Australians indulged a 'passion for perpetual motion, perhaps for fear that we may have to sit down and face reality if we don't keep going'.

Well, quite. That's the attraction, and only Nobel laureates in fiction can unflinchingly face the possibility of too much reality. Like Voss, White's tragic heroic explorer, the runner discovers 'how much less destructive of the personality are thirst, fever, physical exhaustion, much less destructive than people'. But to discover this in running, White would have had to get involved.

So on with the moon-shoes and out on the road. Alone in Manly, free to make it up as I go along, running is like hitting a tennis ball against a wall. I'm in any contest I choose, the Olympic marathon or the lonely front-running stages of the inaugural and imaginary Manly Classic. I'm right on the pace.

In the winter sunshine my shadow tags along. In England he's easily discouraged, but in Australia he makes it every time, though out of shape and in fact not that great a runner. His shoulders are slumped, and his legs move painfully slowly, though I chivvy him along because personally I'm feeling fine.

Another attraction of jogging, if you take the simplest starting point right outside your door, is that it's local. It's a regular tour of the community, just fast enough to avoid well-meaning chat and the more dangerous children. I get to see and be part of wherever it is I'm living, which means occasional dog bites but also the chance to help boys free their fish hooks from the river. Manly is no different, and before long I'm nodding and raising a hand to Manly people I know. Up at the former gasworks Ben Wotton from the Surf Club is doing a mad lung-bursting uphill sprint circuit – he stops long enough to gasp, hands on knees, 'Must be easier ways of earning a beer.' Maria Silva from the rifle club is warming up by the Santova Café, and Bobby Yonks is on the promenade in shorts. He's not running – just off to fetch the paper. And inevitably, like anyone else who runs in Manly, I'm destined sooner or later to be accosted by Billy Kerrigan.

Billy 'Tats' Kerrigan is the very tanned white-haired man I once saw walking backwards along the beach in his youthful Manly swim trunks. I thought he was sixty. He is seventy-four. We meet for the first time when he stops me near the surf club ('Mate! Mate!') and asks for some help. There's a cream he needs to rub on an awkward place on his back. He turns and shows it to me, a raw patch. 'Gotta put this on me cancer, mate,' he says. 'Me! Of all people! Getting cancer!'

It takes years to go brown as Billy is brown. Having skin so deep a colour is itself a sign of age, like the markings or thickness of shell on a tortoise. And without his shirt on, I can see all the tattoos on Billy 'Tats' Kerrigan. He has them on his arms, thighs, calves, on his chest. They are dark blue to black and glistening, melting into his bean-brown skin. They're of women, mostly, with heavy thighs and breasts but on his left upper arm, I'm almost sure, is a tall-masted ship with every sail unfurled.

Billy takes his shirt off at every opportunity, and for a man of seventy-four, he has an astonishing body. He slaps his flat stomach with his hand.

'Look at that, mate. Not bad, eh? God don't make garbage. I was on the scrapheap, I was. I was.'

Billy goes running with Maria Silva at five o'clock in the morning every Tuesday and Saturday. If they see someone else, anyone else, they ask them to tag along, but not just for the fun of it.

'We're training for the pub to pub,' Billy tells me. 'You'd enjoy that, young bloke like you.'

'What is it?'

'It's a race.'

'Thought it might be.'

In Australia, I was never going to escape with simply jogging along. Running can be as competitive as any other Australian sport, and at the 1956 Melbourne Olympics, uniquely in the history of the marathon, a runner was false-started. It requires a particular cast of mind to call back a pack of twenty-six-milers for a premature shuffle at the start. For a different cast of mind, compare the host country's attitude to an earlier Olympic marathon. In 1896, the first race in Greece was measured at 24.85 miles, but for London in 1908 the British imperiously added an extra two miles and 385 yards. This allowed the race to start at Windsor Castle and end in front of the royal box. British priorities were clear, and athletes were not the priority.

'Pub to pub,' Billy says, his face as usual cracking into a smile. He jabs my arm with his fist. 'Piece of cake, mate. You wanna do that, mate.'

The pub to pub is a thirteen-kilometre charity run that follows the coastline north of Manly. This winter the run is in its thirteenth year, and even though Billy Kerrigan is the only man in Australia who's finished it every time, he's almost twice as old as me, and I can see another possible victory. I also like him and want to make him happy so I say of course I'll do it. His face lights up: he's made another convert.

'Good on yer, mate. Ask Maria for the entry form.'

Billy last had a drink forty-one years ago, aged thirty-three, and at AA meetings he gives talks about the importance of keeping occupied. This new religion of running, along with a touch of the old one ('I put my trust in God, Rich') saved Billy Kerrigan from meths and soul implosions on the hilly streets of Sydney. The only traces left are in his face. He has eyes the Australian shade of blue, washed out by sea salt, sunshine and chlorine, but the red rims of his lower eyelids are always visible, as if permanently peeled back from seeing much too much too young.

When his face relaxes it empties, becomes tired and

slightly lost, but Billy rarely relaxes. He has stuff to do: cleaning the surf club, going to an AA meeting, chatting about his wives, not standing still.

'I done a marathon, mate, aged sixty-seven I was. You done one yet? God don't make garbage, Rich. I got loads of medals, mate. You can have one if you like. Take one for the kids. Go on, mate.'

Without events to aim at, from marathons down to five-kilometre fun runs, jogging backslides into a different territory known as 'exercise', dangerously close to walking the dog or pedalling a bike that never leaves the gym. There's no game in that, no play, and despite my temporary defeatism on the beach I find myself agreeing with Australians that competition gives a collective meaning to sport lost if you just bumble about for ever on your own, imagining you're Paula Radcliffe. Yep. Done that too, though not in Manly. The collective meaning is what helps create sport's magic attraction, the tension and redemption that makes addicts of us all.

Maria signs the three of us up for the Newport Arms Pub to Pub thirteen-kilometre race, but knows for a fact that I didn't get many miles in my legs at the rifle club. 'It's not a difficult run,' she promises, 'but you'll need to train.' She laughs her laugh. 'Meet us at the surf club, five a.m. on Saturday.'

There it is again: the Australian application of pressure. *Five o'clock in the morning.* I can't remember the last time I was up that early, for anything. I decide to do some training to prepare for the training, and the next morning I meet Christian Surfer Nic Gilmour running back from Shelly Beach. I do a Billy on him, but Nic can't run the pub to pub because of a pain he has in his side.

'Biblical?'

'Trapezoidal.'

He stretches a bit, then lopes off. Is he whistling? He seems very happy, joyful even, and that's once how I'd imagined myself, alone, content, indifferent to winning and losing. In Manly, this was never going to happen. Already I was joining in, training to race, merging the two different ideas of running that provide the source of conflict in Alan Sillitoe's *The Loneliness of the Long Distance Runner*, always a contradictory book. It's about long, hard cross-country runs, but loved by a generation of school-boys for being short and easy to read.

For Smith, the borstal-boy runner of the title, running is primarily freedom: 'It's a treat, being a long-distance runner, out in the world by yourself with not a soul to make you bad-tempered or tell you what to do.' He can move, he can think, but what he won't do is race to win, even though he's the strongest contender on National Borstal Sports Day. At the climax of the story, he defies the expectations of the middle-class governor (and mine as a middle-class reader) by refusing to win his race.

I take the same attitude into the biggest mass-participation run on earth. This is Australia: there's no shortage of sporting opportunity, and I therefore decide to use Sydney's annual City2Surf as training for my training for Billy's pub to pub. I'm simply slotting into the seasonal unrolling of Australia's sporting inheritance.

Public displays of running, called pedestrianism, were a feature of the early colony, and Australia's star athlete was William Francis 'the Flying Pieman' King. In the 1840s he accepted various challenges, including carrying a seventy-pound dog from Campbeltown to Sydney in eight and a half hours, and a ninety-two-pound live goat (plus an extra twelve pounds) from Sydney to Parramatta. There was money involved, and presumably alcohol, but no one who ever preferred to walk would claim that pedestrianism is sensible.

Accordingly, once a year on a winter Sunday morning, in Sydney's Hyde Park, there assemble Batmen and Robins, men in tutus, leopard-skin chickens, and students in all-over body paint. The City2Surf is open to all-comers, and 60,000 barely dressed people are now milling about before running the fourteen kilometres to Bondi Beach. Some of them have found a free bit of park to jog in, others are stretching, but easily the most common warm-up routine is talking excitedly on a mobile phone ('I'm at the start! Wearing running kit! Where are you?!').

Sydney's City2Surf is very well organised. They take your civilian clothes to Bondi in advance and leave out little cups of water before the start. Many competitors are now carrying these cups as they wander about, arm cocked at a right angle, elbow supported on the other hand, so that today in the Sunday sunshine the centre of Sydney feels like a vast athletic cocktail party.

The lonely long-distance runner would have despised us all. This is running taken over by the contaminated classes, trampled by the bourgeoisie in the idle Sunday hours before brunch. Smith would have cherished his righteousness, forgetting that he was in borstal in the first place because he got things wrong, in his case the hiding place for money from a break-in at a bakery. Later, as he saw it, he was required to offer moral support to the system that sent him down by conforming to expectations and winning a winnable running race. The difference at the City2Surf is that very few of us are expecting to win. That isn't our route to self-respect, to respectability.

Instead, we're expecting to feel pain.

Empire schoolboys, caned into shape with Indian bamboo, learnt early that it was virtuous to suffer without flinching. Naked swimming in April and full-contact boxing would make a man of the most snivelling weasel. Now, if not by the most direct route, popular running has arrived at the same place, where indifference to pain is a virtue. What's the point of walking if it hurts more to run?

This corresponds to a middle-class idea of manliness, a dose of stoicism to add to the responsibility and sense of fair play commonly claimed as virtues for the Empire-bred team sports. In this way, as identified quite correctly by Sillitoe's lonely long-distance runner, sport becomes a territory occupied by the middle class. We hope everyone will be normalised and sanitised by sport – imbued with middle-class values, made middle class. Football hooligans recognise and fight this, medieval brawlers reclaiming something of sport's original energy for themselves, wondering what exactly is wrong with fighting between villages for a head in a sack. They know Sport for All means Middle Class Values for All. So do I, personally preferring hypocrisy and handshakes to a dart in the eye.

In a new country like Australia, freed from the bitterness of centuries of class war, juvenile delinquent Smith might have been persuaded to change his mind. As an Australian, he could have run for himself, and the concept of the fair go for everyone. He'd have been happy to win, would have wanted to prove himself, just as I do now, though if I'm going to end up a winner from 60,000 entrants I need to invent a new category, or carry a live goat. And if anyone else is carrying a goat, I'll have to invent goat categories.

We're set on our way by a starting pistol, for which the

starter had to apply in writing to the Firearms Registry at least six months in advance. Fortunately, this process now allows him to stand high above the crowds, balancing on his various firearms permits. For the first kilometre there's no point trying to run, or even swing my arms, but it's the same for everyone so I've deliberately started as far back as possible. This means that when I do eventually start running, I'm overtaking people all the time, outrunning Australian after Australian like the sweetest of dreams come true.

We run past the Jews for Jesus shop and a drop-in skin cancer clinic, and I overhear spits of conversation, always with the upwards intonation of breathless Australia.

'You can do it?'

Occasionally along the route there are youngsters sitting on the flat roofs of their hot city hangouts, defiantly waving bottles of beer and smoking tabs. They look smug but healthy, as if they have a secret gym habit. And anyway, there aren't that many of them, and their catcalls are drowned out by the frequent drinking stations and the crackle of 60,000 plastic cups splitting underfoot.

The folklore surrounding the City2Surf centres on Heartbreak Hill, a two-kilometre incline climbing to Bondi Junction. A red-faced bloke in a Union Jack boiler suit is walking it. With the Ashes almost upon us, or indeed at any other time, this is fundamentally wrong. If you're going to wear the suit, you have to run the run. If you want to embarrass yourself by walking, wear an Australian flag. Some people have no idea of the most basic facts of life.

As we enter the suburbs stretching down towards Bondi, children have put out tables and drinks in front of their houses. Old gents in deckchairs wave from the pavement and shout, 'See ya next year!'

Definitely. I'm a champ. I come in six thousand eight hundred and fifty-ninth, in a time of 74 minutes 13 seconds, and any time under seventy-five minutes guarantees a start with the leading group next year. I'm chuffed to bits, while recognising that six thousand eight hundred and fifty-ninth is not quite a podium finish. However, this result is before handicapping comes into effect. I need to discount all the women and children who beat me (including a boy of about twelve), and everyone younger than me (even if only by a day). Also those who trained longer or who are more naturally gifted or who were brought up in more conducive circumstances for running, and then I'm almost the winner. In fact, everyone's a winner.

I suffered; we all did. As Saul Bellow once wrote, 'it's too bad, but suffering is about the only reliable burster of the spirit's sleep'. Sport is a toe in the water, a timely reminder, and that's why so many writers find time for it. The Japanese novelist and short-story writer Yukio Mishima was addicted to bodybuilding, and believed physical exertion was part of his 'spiritual hygiene'. He must have missed behind the ears, because he ended his life with a sword in the guts begging a nineteen-year-old Tokyo University student to chop off his head. He called physical effort the 'ultimate verification of existence', but then Mishima-san had a weakness for exaggeration. It's not the ultimate, but it is one, one small verification of existence.

With the City2Surf safely negotiated, and my existence verified, I'm ready to start training for the pub to pub with Maria and Billy Kerrigan. We meet up at five a.m. and run to the Spit Bridge and back. We meet at five a.m. and run to Sydney, crossing the Harbour Bridge not long after dawn. We meet at five a.m. and run to the end of North Head. As a recovering alcoholic, Billy is taking life one day at a time. I suggest he might find this easier if he started every day a bit later.

'Nah, mate, best part of the day. Look at that.'

It's dark, and all I can see as we jog side by side are the street lights on the long hill of Darley Road. We climb past St Patrick's on the left, up past St Paul's School which smells of PE and steak, past Manly Hospital and into the National Park on top of North Head. Maria is running a good distance ahead of us, and Billy is running and talking. Today's mantra is about the toughness of women. 'They're tough, mate, they're tough. Maria has run nine marathons. Nine marathons, mate, how about that? Women are tough, I tell ya. Look at her go, mate. She's only a small thing.'

It is now 5.20 a.m. I can keep up with Billy on the hill – it's the talking that does me in, and as usual when I'm overdoing it I think of Steve Ovett, all tendons and ligaments and teeth. In one of his Olympic years he suffered a knee injury while out training. This is what I always remember, as reported on the nine o'clock news: he ran into a gate. When overexerted I worry about running into gates and busting my knees. I go hazy and understand how something like that could happen.

Back on Manly golf course, I needed to live in the now and resist distractions. Running requires an exactly opposite technique: it's all distraction, and training with Billy I try to think about anything except what I'm actually doing, and how much my legs are aching and my lungs are bleeding and how my internal organs have compacted somewhere above my stomach. The lonely long-distance runner asks, 'I wonder if I'm the only one in the running business with this system of forgetting that I'm running because I'm too busy thinking.'

No, young Smith, you're not. In fact, you should spend less time on your own.

Experienced runners recommend as much dissociative thinking as possible: fight the now, and the poison knowledge that running by choice is a stupid and self-inflicted agony, as non-runners often find time to point out. So why does anyone do it?

Narcissism, self-hatred, primitive courage. Transcendence, as the mind drifts away from the body. It passes the time.

Already we're at the top of the hill and running by the entrance to the old quarantine station, where all infected ships used to stop before being processed to Sydney. These days they offer a walking tour, at night, and the night I took it I got a lift down with an Indian in a turban and his Swedish girlfriend. 'No worries, mate.' My mistake, they were both Australian.

Guy the excellent guide then took us looking for ghosts, and handed out kerosene storm lanterns so that everywhere we went we were accompanied by creaking, one of the great lost noises of the seafaring centuries. The lanterns flared the undersides of the high canopies of gum trees, lace umbrellas against the moonlit sky.

In particular, Guy gave us fair warning about the spirit of the matron in the old quarantine hospital. In any group that entered her ward, he told us, she liked to terrorise the most macho male.

'Who is that?' he asked, stopping suddenly and looking from face to lamp-lit face.

I was hoping it was me, but it wasn't. I never saw any ghosts at all.

The spirits in the quarantine station encourage rumination about life and death, or as anyone brought up on the King James Bible knows, the quick and the dead. We accelerate and head out through the park towards the end of North Head, but the dead are not so easily distanced.

North Head, Manly, is where within six months of the arrival of the First Fleet, the Aboriginal Kay-e-my-gal people came to die.

'It was truly shocking to go round the coves of this harbour,' wrote Captain John Hunter of the *Sirius*, 'which were formerly so much frequented by the natives; where, in the caves of the rocks, which used to shelter whole families in bad weather, were now to be seen men, women, and children, lying dead. As we had never yet seen any of these people who have been in the smallest degree marked with the small-pox we had reason to suppose they have never before now been affected by it.'

At dawn, the bushland of North Head reminds me of Ku-ring-gai Chase. There's a sense of human insufficiency, and running feels like a doomed attempt to approximate a guess at an Aboriginal harmony between body, mind and the great outdoors. If the English cringe recreationally before Australians, modern Australians cringe spiritually before Aborigines, who once knew the secrets of the land.

This isn't much consolation to Rick Shapter, Manly's Aboriginal Heritage Officer, who has a desk in the Town Hall, itself a landscape statement from early in the last century. It has white pillars either side of the doorway in provincial courthouse style, the kind of place Gregory Peck would come to defend the innocent. In a film. Rick is another huge man, tall rather than broad, and he sweeps out into the public lobby wearing a sports jacket, the old English type in herringbone grey and green. He has an earring, a goatee, and his long red face has eyes as blue as Billy Kerrigan's.

It's madness to try and guess, or worse, think you *can* guess, where Australians come from by how they look.

'My other mob's from Devon,' Rick says, as we settle in at one of the public tables, 'and there's some Scottish in there too.'

I'd been meaning to ask about Manly and traditional Aboriginal sports, but Rick isn't a great deal of help.

'There's only a certain amount I can tell you.'

This isn't because part of Rick is from Devon, but because his Aboriginal mob originated in another part of Australia. This is one consequence of the British Australian policy of dispersal – most Aborigines now find themselves in the wrong place. Like Trinity Bay, the only Aborigine buried in Manly Cemetery, who in 1891 aged seventeen died from pneumonia after catching a chill during a game of rugby. Trinity was named after the beach near Cairns in Queensland where he was found, apparently abandoned. He was then brought down south by the Christian charity of a Dr Sachs, of Manly.

This story is one of many. The songs Trinity Bay knew about the Queensland landscape were of no use to him here in New South Wales. The Manly stories to explain Manly had been lost with the smallpox, or dispersed elsewhere. The culture fragmented as Aboriginal people were separated from their places of birth, losing along the way their songs and route maps and moral codes.

The last references to an Aboriginal lifestyle in Manly date from 1829. After that, the 1830s were a time of furrowed debate about whether Aborigines were human. Local historian Pauline Curby calls this 'a difficult time for Aborigines', and Anthony Trollope after his first visit in 1871 was equally understated: 'There has been some rough work.'

The Sydney suburbs are as Aboriginal as Alice Springs. If that's harder to recognise, it's because the shock of disease and oppression and dispersal was most effective here, in this place where tribes gathered together, because it was here, like the European invaders, they preferred to live. North Head, Manly, is one of the most important indigenous sites in Australia. There's a rich source of high-quality ochre. There are rock engravings. In the spring, it's a great place for having a picnic and watching the migration of whales, but no one now can be sure, without the knowledge passed down through generations, exactly why North Head was chosen for corroborees and gatherings. If anyone did know, they probably wouldn't say.

'That's why there's only a certain amount I can tell you.'

Rick Shapter can tell me he's a former national-level pentathlete, and he tells me about Japanese imperial history, and the philosophies of the ancient Greeks. But he can't and won't tell me the larger part of what he knows about Aboriginal life – the belief systems or the exact location of many sacred sites.

'For the most studied people on earth,' he says, and I notice he has some kind of delicate cancer or polyp on his left lower eyelid, which often trembles with suppressed anger, 'the concept of "need to know" has been a great defence.'

This elective silence is a blunt rejection of precious

Western assumptions. It's as if there's no inherent virtue in shared knowledge, let alone openness or transparency. As Rick says, the solidarity of Aboriginal secrecy fights the 'European imperative to destroy what it doesn't understand'.

There are special enemies, anthropologists and ethnologists, travel writers. The Aborigines, Rick says, try to ignore them, or when that doesn't work they tell jokes.

Two Aborigines meet up deep in the Gibson Desert.

'Mate, how are ya?'

'Dunno mate. Have to check with my anthropologist.'

In Greenland the Inuit people have developed, quite independently, the same gag. Academics overexcited by their own dedication, and Rick picks out for special mention the French and Germans, don't laugh. They want the secret rituals, the hidden codes.

'So I tell them one of the male initiate's secret activities is washing up,' Rick explains, and at this point Monsieur le Professeur wriggles at the probability of an imminent promotion to the Académie française. 'That's why you never see them doing it.'

Rick must know that the lure of secret knowledge, of a withheld path to enlightenment, is immensely seductive. That's why we keep poking about and asking questions. The Aborigines may have the answer, or may have had it, and Rick is right, our first instinct, my first instinct, is to wonder how I can get that off him.

He hints at what we don't know. Each dreaming story is a kind of map of the landscape. Retold on a need-to-know basis, the story can act as a warning or an instruction. These are the two levels widely known and understood. Then there's a third version of each story that provides a moral code, and finally, at the fourth and deepest level and only for initiates, a revelation. These stories cover every inch of the landscape of Australia, every pitch, rink, golf course and oval, because in 60,000 years of pedestrianism, Aborigines have set foot everywhere.

We understand, by instinct, that nature orients us, and not just physically. It can work more grandly than that, as in the holiday awe routinely evoked by mountains and lakes, seascapes. We feel there's some higher truth in natural beauty, in being outside, and this may also explain some of the attraction of running. Outside, jogging along, we're gently keeping in touch.

Shelly Beach is a popular destination for Manly joggers, the end point of a tarmacked continuation of the promenade that curves beyond the surf club and around the first rocky outcrops of the ocean-facing North Head foreshore. The pathway was originally built to hide a sewer pipe, and the first time I ran along it I supposed 'Shelley Beach' had some connection with the romantic poet. Probably, I thought, as the waves crashed in and North Head loomed above, with Shelley and the romantic idea that man is nothing and nature will always prevail. I learnt this at school in English, but I should have paid more attention in biology.

At the deepwater ocean outfalls for Manly's sewage, off the coast of North Head, deformed fish have been found recording up to 250 times normal levels of benzene hexachloride. I don't know what this is, but I don't fancy it with chips, and nor do the people of Manly, who come out in their thousands in protests organised by POOO (People Opposed to Ocean Outfalls).

Nature will not prevail, not necessarily, and we need to protect what's left. Shelly Beach, with Australian direct-ness, was named that way because it was once covered in shells. Now there are none. That's why I made the mistake about Shelley. As an apology for the missing shellfish, the ocean around the beach is now a protected aquatic reserve, a hopeful sanctuary for elegant wrasse and the weedy seadragon.

I ask Rick if there are any penalties in the Aboriginal belief system for altering or destroying the landscape. 'What might happen, just as an example, to a golf-course designer?'

'Well you know what they say,' Rick shrugs, 'his karma ran over his dogma.'

'And does the karma keep ticking over until it runs over his children's dogma?'

'Could do,' Rick says.

It's another secret.

In the absence of Aboriginal secret knowledge, weighed down by history, we have to find our own spiritual way. Running can be part of that attempt, and one of the first people to explore this was the Australian running coach Percy Cerutty ('Pronounced like sincerity,' Percy enjoyed saying, 'but without the sin'). A sickly adult, Percy Cerutty decided to improve his health by trying out athletics in 1942, at the age of forty-seven, and his name would now be universally known if it wasn't for Sir Roger Bannister.

For a while, at the beginning, everything went well. Using his body as a live experiment, Percy developed a creed of physical and spiritual renewal through running, and in 1947 he finished a marathon in 3 hours 2 minutes, just failing to qualify for the London Olympics. He was fifty-two.

He embraced the ascetic, pre-industrial aspect of

running, appreciating its simplicity. You can't buy a present for a runner – I tried to get something for Maria, who'd helped me more than anyone to find my way around Manly (I couldn't buy her a gun, and Luke in Northside Runners admitted that if she already had shoes and clothes there wasn't much else I could get her for running). It's a sport not easily commodified or corrupted, and Cerutty made a virtue of this by developing his belief that running could explore, in a practical and physical way, spiritual possibilities like the union of mind and body. It was a path, not an end in itself, an experience in the quest for clarity. In that sense, running was a form of yoga, a method of striving to reach beyond ourselves.

Cerutty's first steps were more practical. He nailed a sign to the front of his house at Yarra, Victoria – 'Percy Wells Cerutty – Conditioner of Men'. Then he set up some weights and renamed his back garden: 'The International Athletics Centre'. He plotted some training routes over the local dunes, and combined his vague spiritual ideas with the physical pain of hard running on soft sand.

It seemed to work. Percy's best-known runner was Herb Elliott, undefeated over a mile and Olympic champion when he retired in 1962 at the age of twenty-four. By that time, however, Cerutty's reputation had already been determined by John Landy, his first great protégé, who in 1954 battled Roger Bannister to break the four-minute barrier for a mile. Landy trained on the dunes, sucked in Cerutty's philosophy, and made it – he ran a sub-four-minute mile and broke Bannister's world record. Unfortunately, he was seven weeks too late.

After that, and despite Herb Elliott's later success, Cerutty's career was forever stalled at the fork of the road untravelled, always at what might have been. A victory for Landy could have triggered the Recreational Cringe a generation earlier, and made Percy for life. For the rest of his days, as the coach of the Australian who broke the four-minute mile, he could have spoken more softly and still been heard.

Dismissed during his lifetime as shrill and eccentric, his ideas are now curiously suited to modern jogging. For most of us, and probably 59,500 of the competitors at Sydney's *City2Surf*, success doesn't depend on oxygen intake or split-lap times, but, well, let Percy tell it himself: 'I am convinced that *movement is life* – activity in the human regenerates, *makes* for life.' He decided his followers would be called Stotans, a merging of Stoics and Spartans, and attempted to elevate the refusal to quit into a philosophy. To one of his younger runners he wrote, 'You will only surpass me in *speed*, not in the effort or endurance or striving or ability to take punishment.'

It's no coincidence that Percy Cerutty, who came to running as I did in middle age, developed ideas that are instantly comprehensible to a middle-aged runner like me. If I was younger, I'd try to be faster. As I'm not, I shall simply try harder, with the effort as important as the effect. And when I suffer, like Percy I can believe that suffering is an important feature of sport. If it wasn't, we'd have cut it out by now, and be left with nothing more painful than cribbage and beer.

Percy Cerutty didn't always express himself as clearly as he might have done, but then he was in no particular hurry. On his diet of raw vegetables and nuts ('Marry me!' he said to his second wife. 'You'll never have to cook again!'), aged eighty, still running up sandhills, he started enthusiastically on a new book called *Why Die?* It proposed that physical self-mastery could reverse the most stubborn laws of nature, though sadly he never finished writing it. He died.

Many people thought Percy a couple of hurdles short of the full 400 metres, but he started us off towards what we are now, Stotan joggers one and all. Percy Cerutty anticipated the quest for our true nature on the pavements.

In other ways he was less enlightened, and it may be just as well that Percy remains a marginal figure. Inside his copy of compatriot Germaine Greer's *The Female Eunuch*, he wrote, 'I know what this woman needs.'

A good run, presumably.

Because, as every worthy Victorian knows (and not just Percy Cerutty) sport is food for the soul. The healthy body is a visible sign of the healthy mind, a physical complement to the moral development of character. On its own, however, physical exertion is never enough, true manliness the harmonious growth of body *and* mind, creating the strong of limb and the pure of heart. Unless, that is, the Victorians had it altogether wrong. Sport is not virtue; it may even be its opposite, with mud and slime on, in the rain.

Instead of improving Australians as people, sport may be making them worse, princes into frogs. There's evident and illiberal danger, for example, in believing too closely the media stereotypes of ultimate winners and losers. An artificially generated dislike of strangers seems unhelpful, and now as always sport can serve as a shrink-to-fit disguise for extremes of chauvinism and nationalism. The swimmers Durack and Wylie resisted and triumphed; the Aboriginal cricketer Jack Marsh never had a chance.

This dystopic view of sport, at the other end of the track from Muscular Christianity or Percy Cerutty, is expressed most forcefully in a French experimental novel. Yes, really.

George Perec's *W or The Memory of Childhood* (1975) is partly set on a tiny island off Tierra del Fuego, named W after its founder Wilson, perhaps 'the leader of a group of convicts who mutinied during transportation to Australia'.

> What is true, what is certain, what is immediately striking, is that W, today, is a land where Sport is king, a nation of athletes where sport and life unite in a single magnificent effort.

That rings some bells. Perec then explores the logic of a 'sports morality', imagining a land in thrall to the Olympic ideal, the values of sport adopted to the exclusion of all others. The loser in a running race 'has to run an extra lap with his shoes on back to front', or later, as the society evolves, have his dismembered loser's corpse hung out to dry on meat hooks. 'However,' Perec continues, 'the unequal treatment of winners and losers is far from being the only example of the systematic injustice in life on W'.

The sports state of W becomes a tyranny of chance and the 'permanent strife' of athletes fighting to win a name for themselves. 'The wish to overtake or overcome others' is nurtured and encouraged until the athlete-citizens know no other way of existing.

> That's what there is, and that's all. There are competitions every day, where you Win and Lose. You

have to fight to live. There is no alternative. It is not possible to close your eyes to it, it is not possible to say no. There's no recourse, no mercy, no salvation to be had from anyone.

This is a vision of sporting values isolated and exposed, the consequence of the kind of 'coming second is first loser' mentality that can give sport a bad name, especially if that attitude becomes public policy. In Australia, the government-sponsored sports academy system is usually credited, along with the weather, for Australia's sporting ascendancy.

The Australian Institute of Sport (AIS), a hothouse academy for elite athletes, was set up with federal funding in 1981. The training programmes were originally limited to eleven foundation sports, including vote-winners like athletics and cricket. There was also weightlifting, less surprising than it seems because the AIS had been paying close attention to the sporting example of the German Democratic Republic.

The author of *Australia's Sporting Success, The Inside Story* is a career Australian sports administrator called John Bloomfield (former chairman of the AIS, co-chairman of the Australian Sports Commission, president of Sports Medicine Australia). He spent eight years in the 1960s observing 'at first hand a large number of the sophisticated programs' already in place in the communist bloc, and acknowledges the influence these systems had on the sporting development of Australia.

The National Talent Search Program, for example, to identify children likely to win at Sydney 2000 (the target was sixty medals) was based on an Eastern European model. Ninety-nine per cent of children failed the tests

(Australia won fifty-eight medals). The psychologists were equally in awe. AIS veteran Brian Miller of *Gold Minds*, the book that didn't improve my golf, calmly writes that 'during the 1970s and the 1980s the East German system was arguably the most effective in world sport'. He admits that he's a 'great fan' of the successful East German approach to motivation, which included, if anyone needs reminding, a shoot-to-kill policy for athletes tempted by an unscheduled cross-city break.

Not even Mike at the beach would say this was all good.

We're now copying the academy system in Britain, as one way of avoiding the inexact science of entrusting athletes to hit-and-miss gurus like Percy Cerutty. Individual coaches, in any case, can be overrated. The brilliant Manly swimmer Boy Charlton was coached by a Manly shoe salesman who livened up the sea voyage to the Stockholm Olympics by jumping fully-clothed into the middle of the Indian Ocean. The man had previously suffered shell shock on the Western Front, but when Charlton and the Olympic swim team set out for Europe he was fine. Perhaps someone took him aside in a motivational huddle, and said the key word. Trenches.

Initially centralised in Canberra, the AIS was quaintly nicknamed Fortress Bruce, though it now has outposts all over the country. The nearest to Manly is the Sydney Academy of Sport, a short trip up Pittwater Road and then turn left inland. I soon discover it isn't served by public transport. That's because it's an elite institution – the public aren't supposed to go there. I therefore have to jog it, running into the bush along the hard shoulder of the Wakehurst Parkway, watching my feet to avoid discarded pie trays and dried-out lizards.

The Sydney Academy of Sport is a A$47 million self-contained multi-sport campus with a A\$6 million operating budget. However much this is, in the opinion of the government it's too much. That why they've brought in Chris Mamo, young, compact, dapper, the newly appointed client service co-ordinator in a pressed white shirt and dark trousers. He makes me feel more sweaty than I am.

Chris, once a triathlete and still with that tight-skinned look of extreme fitness, gives me the tour.

First impressions are of immaculate grass rugby pitches dotted with scraps of bandage and flattened orange peel. The Manly Warringah Sea Eagles rugby league team have made the academy their training base, and Chris tells me that Western Force, the new Super 14 rugby union franchise, have also been training here. There's no sign of them now, only a couple of girls in netball skirts chucking a rugby ball to each other. A wheelchair rugby team is staying in the residential motel, and like anyone else who books in, they can use the swimming pool, the indoor sports hall, the footie pitches, the running track, the kayaking lake, and the overhead rope courses.

Or at least that used to be the case. The campus is now prickly with risk management issues. If the academy gets it wrong, this pleasant attentive man called Chris will go to jail.

'And I'm not prepared to let that happen,' Chris Mamo says, quite reasonably, I feel.

In the twenty-five-metre pool, nine-year-old champs are hammering it up and down. They're so fit they don't stop to breathe. The weights gym has stainless-steel racks and spring-loaded traps, the familiar instruments of torture. There's a Sports Medicine Centre with six doctors, none of them obviously on duty, and a boating lake with no boats on it. There are cricket nets with bowling machines, and a lone batsman getting his eye in with some crisp off drives, the only sound to pock the silence other than escaped compressed air, which we follow to the indoor sports hall where tyres are being pumped for specialist rugby wheelchairs.

Chris Mamo is a little embarrassed. 'The academy has 350 beds,' he says, as if I should imagine what it might be like if they were full. At the end of an empty corridor, a wheelchair glides silently by. 'In the Sports Science Lab there's a VO$_2$ Max machine. Come and see the Sports Science Lab.'

The machine that goes bleep adds value. For A$360 they'll clip you in and 'trode you up and report back on the rate you put hairs on your chest. I consider giving it a go, but can't see the merit in accurately assessing my physical decline.

Basically, the Sydney Academy of Sport has loads of high-quality sports-centre-type stuff, but on this particular sunny winter afternoon only the pool is being used with any sense of urgency. I know, of course, why this is. Everyone in Manly is much too busy competing to have time for training and testing. Some grumpy teenagers get dropped off by their mums, and then some rosy-faced boys who by this time next year will be grumpy teenagers. It must be a delicate alchemy to change a love of games into a love of winning, without killing the love of games.

'This isn't quite the relentless, well-oiled sporting machine I was expecting.'

'Far from it,' Chris says solemnly. 'Far from it.'

There are money problems. A new track has to be laid at a cost of A$300,000, and non-elite athletes will now be charged A$4.50 a time. Today on the track there's one middle-aged gent, and he hasn't paid. He arrives every day promptly at 3.29, just before the gate attendant at half past.

Chris tells me that whenever an economic squeeze comes on, sport is the first to suffer. I'm not convinced this is true. Every department thinks their own budget is the first to go, from education through parks to the arts. I failed to get picked for England in the '80s, for example, or to stage my first neo-concrete opera, because in both cases the Thatcher cutbacks decimated my potential government funding.

But Chris is going to put things right by increasing corporate bonding days and team-building seminars. This explains the overhead ropeways, like obstacle courses eighty feet in the air. On an increasingly regular basis, men and women in suits will be pushed to their limits for the benefit of their company's accountancy department. Selling the idea that sport and physical activity offers an education, Chris wants to hire out the boats and the pool and the sports hall, with the ropeways kept in reserve for pen-pushers who thought they were coming for fun.

'We're leaning more towards the hospitality and leisure industry,' Chris explains. 'That's the way we're going.'

The Sydney Academy of Sport, envy of the British sporting establishment, is now confident of nurturing the next generation of high-performing human resources managers. This sounds like the beginning of the end, bronze medal at best. What a heartening discovery. The outer tentacles of the Australian Institute of Sport are beginning to shrivel, to retreat. This is excellent news.

I think. It *is* good news, I'm almost sure of it. If the

Australians take their eye off the ball, we can expect a fairer contest in the future. But as I'm running back towards Manly, kicking up lizards and aluminium pie tins, I'm worried. This may be a cunning Australian plan to rob us of our most durable excuse for losing.

The Australian Institute of Sport, its lavish government funding and unquestioned status and unremitting excellence, was supposed to be proof of Australia's sporting obsession. That's why they always win. They're obsessed – there's something wrong with them, and what's more, as Patrick White kindly articulated on our behalf, Australia's infatuation with sport inhibits the country's development in other areas.

He meant culture. Smugly, insufferably, we always used to assume that however miserable our latest defeat on the sports field, we could beat the Australians at culture. That's why we grew up with Clive James and Germaine Greer. They came over to beat the English at their oldest games, wit and argument and writing, and they succeeded. But at least we made them come over, back when they were the ones with the Cringe. Now I was the one who had to travel, for the same reason, because these days there's little solace in the fading British talent for levitation.

Former generations simply rose above it: they beat the Australians by refusing to make winning an objective. George Orwell was comfortably above such vulgarity, as were many of the competitors themselves, like 'Plum' Warner and perhaps even David Gower. The Australians, however, were desperate to win every time, a sporting asset but a human frailty.

There are English patriots who devote otherwise useful lives to the memory of Greg Chappell instructing brother

Trevor to bowl underarm to close out a one-day cricket match. The Australians are obsessed, they're *unhinged*. This psychological disorder allows England to lose and yet still remain superior. We don't care so much. But personally I do care, a lot. That's why I'm in Australia doing my utmost in Manly.

And, so far, I'd have to say that Manly doesn't feel like a totalitarian sporting dystopia. After jogging back from the academy, I shower and change, put on my best shirt and my golfing trousers, and go out to look for Manly people not making sacrifices for their sport, sane human beings who have no intention of simulating trench warfare until their biceps tear off at the tendon. Basically, is there life without sport in the suburb of Manly? Without sport, what on earth would people like me be doing?

As an adolescent, my difficult phase coincided with fighting on the rugby pitch and occasionally losing interest in sport altogether. When that happened, it seemed preferable to mime guitar for the benefit of a toilet mirror. A bit cramped, but it was the only room in the house with a lockable door. Rock star was a fleeting passion simmered on the smokeless fuel of *Top of the Pops* and a poster of the Pretenders, but unlike playing for England the dream didn't last, even though the chances of making it were probably better. I used to imagine I could survive at Twickenham on the wing in an England international dominated by the forwards. Or at Wembley as goalkeeper in an England 7–0 rout of Latvia. I *know* I could have cut it on stage at the Hammersmith Palais, bashing the tambourine.

At the Old Manly Boatshed, it's Songwriters' Live night, and first up is Mike, a prop forward with an acoustic guitar. I think he's great, even though in a cellar with thirty other people who know Mike by name, this must be Third Division at best. It makes me wonder why singer-songwriters on the telly, in the Premier League, get paid so much.

Mike can do entertainment and he can do acoustic melancholy. I sit there and get gently stewed on red wine and listen to how, in Australia too, nobody understands the pain. My mind wanders to what happens next after my wife and children are wiped out in a plane crash. Then Mike's smiling and bowing, and chugging a beer as if worse things happen at sea.

He's followed by an electric three-piece band with a lip-out guitar-playing lead singer, of the kind that used to live in my mirror. Like all the best rockers he moves like an athlete, and he has the same shoes as me. I check, and he does, because after all we're not so different. He's a pub rocker like I'm a pub footballer: more ambitious than at first it might seem. He's playing Old Manly Boatshed but also the Hollywood Bowl, and so is his bass player, who, like every bass player ever, took up the instrument to avoid having to dance. It shows.

I don't know if the lads are anti-sport, but they sing an upbeat indie number about getting lost in the Louvre ('It just goes on and on and on/And all the paintings look the same') called 'Virgin and Child'. I can sympathise with this feeling, and I like the title, but Australia is really beyond saving if Manly culture is a mixture of all-day sport and pub rock which slags off European art galleries.

It isn't.

If it was, Kate Grenville wouldn't be drawing a crowd to Manly Library on a midweek night in winter.

As a writer, Kate Grenville can give me a right proper

hiding, both home and away. She's a scratch handicapper and former winner of the Orange Prize, Britain's richest book award. She has corkscrew Janet Frame hair and is talking about her new novel to an audience of about fifty people. It is not a manly occasion; in fact I'm the only young man there, and I'm not a young man.

Kate was born in Manly, and *The Secret River* is a historical epic about early settlers on the Hawkesbury River, just north of here. At the beginning of the reading, she asks for a show of hands from those descended from convicts. Enthusiastically, about twelve or thirteen of the older ladies shoot up their hands.

'I'll be checking your bags on the way out.'

Kate cracks her gig gag, her icebreaker, and then reminds us that even fifteen years ago very few people would have volunteered this information. She tells the story of the famous catalogue in Sydney's Mitchell Library which had a name card for every Australian who arrived in chains. Pretending an idle curiosity or some vital research, Australians from all over the country would travel to Sydney and search the catalogue for the card with their family's name on it. Then, when no one was looking, they'd boldly shuffle the card into a handbag or deep suit pocket, to be destroyed as soon as conveniently possible. Everyone knows this – it's the story most often told to illustrate the shame of the Taint, the Stain.

'Only thing is,' Kate says brightly, 'this catalogue in the Mitchell Library never existed.'

The main character in *The Secret River* is William Thornhill, transported from London for stealing wood. He is loosely based on one of Kate Grenville's ancestors, and after the reading I ask about her research. I imagine Kate standing on the banks of the Thames, and wonder whether she felt anger or resentment against nineteenth-century London, or all England.

'Against the class distinctions.'

William Thornhill is not well treated by the authorities, and is sneered at by the lords and ladies he ferries across the river.

'And now?'

'I mean now. It's still there.'

'In the publishing world?'

'As soon as you open your mouth you get the snide jokes about convicts.'

I'm shocked. I *am* shocked. I thought this type of foolishness only survived in Ian Botham and the Tavern Stand at Lord's. For an antidote, I go for a drink afterwards with Heather and Kimberley. They're about my age, and we decide on the roof bar at the Steyne Hotel, where I ask them about unmanly pursuits in this seaside capital of sports. Is culture endangered by sport, and its heavily advertised day-night shadow?

'You just have to be resigned to it,' Heather says, looking down through the crenellated brickwork at the Norfolk pines, and then the moonlit ocean.

'How do you mean?'

'I once had a boyfriend who liked windsurfing. I used to phone up the weather to find out when I was going to see him.'

There's a folk singer in the enclosed bar behind us. Presumably she too is resigned to the running triathlete on the screen beside her head, competing for everyone's attention.

Kimberley and Heather are funny and nicely sceptical, and we chat about Kate Grenville and boys 'n' girls and whether a Manly anti-sports movement is more or less likely than several other unlikely things we think up, like England beating Australia at cricket or a Manly affordable for single mothers.

'Long live the LSNFSA,' Heather says defiantly, raising a clenched fist.

'Mmmm.' I have no idea what she's talking about.

'The Liberate Saturday Nights from Sport Association.'

'What's that?'

'I don't know. I've just invented it.'

'Only Saturdays?' Kimberley asks.

'We have to start somewhere.'

And because nothing seems impossible in Australia, Heather talks about mobilising as many people as she can for a barbecue this Saturday night on her lawn. To prove that it's a truly alternative occasion, she even threatens to show her holiday slides.

'I'll get back to you,' she says, but before we go our separate ways Kimberley recommends a book. She's a Buddhist, and this book contains a chapter by a guru who lives in Balgowlah, a neighbouring suburb to Manly. He teaches Zen enlightenment. Through golf.

In Manly there's no shortage of cultural pursuits, even if sport is never far away. In an art shop on the Pittwater Road the artist in residence Patrick – big, fit-looking, shaven-headed and with a bottle of beer in his hand – thinks sport may sometimes stifle artistic activity. But he's also a ski instructor and plays tennis so he's hardly the person to know. At A$25 an hour, learning to paint with Patrick is more expensive than golf.

'Yeah,' he says, 'mate, but at the end of it you get something to stick on the wall.'

I'm about to ask if he can come to our inaugural LSNFSA barbecue (with holiday snaps), but ten-year-old Ruby is dragging him back into the studio because she wants to paint forty flowers.

Manly has three bookshops – one of them the chain behind Kate Grenville's visit – but easily the best is a second-hand shop called Desire Books. Australians are supposed to buy more books per head than any other nation on earth. Another competition won, the podium, the gold medal, but imagine your favourite books, then the books you've been meaning to read, and finally hundreds of books you've just realised you wouldn't mind having a look at. This is Desire Books in Manly, miraculously free of both rubbish and books you think you ought to read but don't really want to.

Adam and Zane, the two thirty-one-year-olds who run it, like chess. It's the 'sport of the mind', they tell me, and they play up to thirty games a week, sitting in the back of the shop and whispering 'You nasty piece of work' at each other as they slide and check the pieces. In the summer they keep the shop open late on Thursday nights, for book lovers and chess players, and get five or six games going on tables out on the pavement.

'I need mental stimulation,' Zane says. 'I need chess. Fancy a game?'

'Hold on, hold on,' I say.

I was supposed to be finding out about cultural activity in Manly, and whether it was stifled by sport, like Patrick the artist suggested.

'It does dissipate something,' Adam says, and winces at his isolated bishop. 'Not that we're necessarily against it. Most things are better than going to the pub and getting pissed and angry.'

'So would you say you're competitive people?'

'Shit yeah,' Zane says. 'I get angry. I get elated. And if I lose, I feel like I've failed in my life's mission.'

If that's what it's like for bookish Manly chess heads, imagine the mood in the half-time changing rooms below the single stand at Manly Oval.

My only cultural disappointment is Manly Art Gallery, showing standard government-funded rubbish 'designed to explore communication and distance by linking artists across Australia, and commissioning them to make a "co-operative" work of art'. The resulting artworks are so sterile they have no observable relation to life, and therefore sport (unless, feeling generous and attracted to human move-ment of any kind, the Australian public enjoy the spectacle of their artists grabbing the money and running).

Never mind, Manly can expect better at its annual arts festival in September. After the Old Manly Boatshed and Kate Grenville and art workshops and Desire Books and the Manly Art Gallery, it's clear that Manly isn't like Swindon or King's Lynn – in need of a one-off yearly festival or risk having no culture to speak of at all.

Not that sport and art were ever genuinely in oppo-sition. They don't, by their nature, exclude each other. Why should they? They don't in me.

I feel a fraud helping to start the Liberate Saturday Nights from Sport Association, so I ring up Heather to tell her I'm not sure it's such a good idea.

'Too late,' she says. 'Barbecue's already cancelled.'

Heather had quite a few people lined up but then, one by one, they started dropping out. The first meeting of the LSNFSA clashed with the opening match of Tri-Nations rugby. No can do.

'Never mind,' Heather says. 'Maybe we should think smaller. Start out by liberating Tuesday nights.'

* * *

Which seems more plausible, and better for my health because I can now have an early night before Sunday's pub to pub. It starts at eight in the morning, so a long lie-in for Billy and Maria, who the next day are bouncing up and down at Dee Why Beach at least an hour before the start.

Australia is famous for the impeccable staging of major sporting events. They're not bad at minor sporting events, either, and the clothes are again going ahead by truck and the organisers have even sprung a surprise (at least to me). The first kilometre of the race is to be run on Dee Why Beach, on the kind of murderous soft sand made the source of all virtue by Percy Cerutty.

I split up with Billy and Maria, agreeing to meet them after the finish, and for reasons of morale I discreetly slip towards the back of the field. As we set off, about 1,500 of us sliding and sinking in the fine yellow sand, I let the front runners build up a lead. You go on ahead, I think; I'll catch up with you later. I don't mean in a running sense, because despite the shrillness of sports commentary and the insistence of twisted Nike ads, to get the most from sport you have to give up on excellence. At some stage you do. Otherwise, if you believe that winning is everything, sport is going to come as a big disappointment.

That doesn't mean I've given up trying, even though I'm not trying to win. And this morning, especially on the soft sand, everyone around me is audibly trying their hardest, panting, cursing, as full of never-say-die attitude as anyone at the AIS. The difference is, everyone can enter the Newport Arms Pub to Pub, and get to the start on a bus, too. A wide variety of people have done just that, and struggling along beside me there are Swiss-Australian dynamos and huge Fijian-Australian hulks, there's Maria and Billy, and Mona, who we somehow picked up on one of our regular five a.m. training runs. She was out for an early-morning walk, maybe to fetch the milk.

'Yeah, come on, mate,' Billy said. 'Run with us.'

Mona is Australian, and has been for thirty-one years, but she's also Egyptian. This is irrelevant and very interesting, one story among many that are coming together, just briefly, for a morning's sporting entertainment.

On their frequent tours of England, Australian national teams give a false sense of Australian stability. Here they come again, in their green and gold or their baggy green caps. Nothing has changed since last time. They're tough and determined and here to win.

But in fact Australia is always changing. Between our loss of the Ashes in 1989 and our attempt to win them back in 2005, nearly two million new immigrants arrived in Australia at the rate of over a hundred thousand a year. That's 10 per cent of the population, and a varied mix is out for the pub to pub, as well as a full range of ages and sizes. Most of us, wherever we come from, are in need of some trickery to keep us going, and there are printed signs fixed to lamp posts along the route. They shout 'PUB FUN', and then, a little lower down, as if this was the trick, or the joke, 'RUN'.

If you're truly competitive, it doesn't matter who you're up against. I find myself running with Joe Fisher, originally from New Zealand, who is 6 foot 2 inches tall. I offer to take the lead. I am 5 foot 10 inches tall, and with Joe right behind me I can't resist running under branches that hang roughly to 5 foot 11. He soon drops away.

The big question in these races is then how to pace yourself. As a general rule, never assume you can overtake joggers who look like the kind of joggers you ought to be able to overtake. In that sense, running is a model of liberal attitudes – no one can tell by sex or age or even running style how relentlessly any individual can keep trogging along for the full thirteen kilometres. Instead, look at what they're wearing. If you find yourself running beside someone in a colour-coordinated synthetic super-wicking jogging outfit, you're going too fast. If you're next to a man with change jangling in his pocket and a dog on a lead, and he's turning into his house on the way back from the shops, you probably need to get a move on.

Otherwise, as long as you keep your head busy, your legs and lungs will take care of themselves. I get through half a kilometre thinking about the 30,000 condoms used in two weeks at the Sydney Olympic village. Then I'm brought back to reality by my aching knees, and wonder if this is good for me. Not for my soul, obviously, which glows in the dark. I mean my flesh and bones, because earlier generations were less impressed by the virtues of keeping fit. Even the lonely long-distance runner, young enough for borstal, is already imagining a retirement 'through old age at thirty-two because of lace curtain lungs, a football heart, and legs like varicose beanstalks'.

This is a boy in his 1950s prime, remember, and rereading the story I'm shocked to discover his daily run is five miles long. *Five miles*. That's nothing. In the fifty years between then and now the general reading public has developed a taste for ten-kilometre dashes, half-marathons, marathons. Fell-running. For modern audiences with enjoyable memories of long distance fun-runs, Sillitoe's story should be renamed. *The Mixed-Upness of the Middle-Distance Runner*.

I'm past five miles already, and happy to be going at whatever pace I seem to be going. Think of something

175

your mind off the aches and pains because not
them these days is new; after a certain age there are
old or new injuries, just the same injuries all the time
in rotation.

Jogging along, of the now but not in it, I notice some
skywriting and assume it's an advert. Another kilometre
eaten up by wondering about skywriting as a marketing
strategy in England. Like junk mail, maybe it happens all
the time even though it doesn't work. There are messages
in the English sky as regular as Reader's Digest Prize
Draws, but we rarely get to see them because they're
hidden behind clouds. Today, the message in the
Australian sky reads 'SIN'.

I wonder why we're here. Not here existentially, but out
here competing on a Sunday morning, or making the time
and effort for any sport, and I imagine it's the same for
Australians as it is for everyone else. There's company, the
escape from domesticity, and keeping fit (otherwise
known as living for ever). Some people are bullied into it,
others are ambitious, or it's in the family, a habit, or an
obligation after once promising someone something
sometime late in a pub. There are men and women
defying age, or running because it's cheaper than anything else. At least one person here, out of fifteen
hundred, must be repressing excess aggression or an
overactive sex drive. Others might be masochists. All
these motives are possible, but once you've started, in a
contest of any kind, the important thing is not to stop.

Whatever the shape or age of the face, the Australians
alongside me in the pub to pub have the indomitable
crease-eyed squint of the cricketer Don Bradman. It's the
sun that does it, chiselling that Bradman twenty-two-yard
stare that settles on Australian faces as soon as anyone's

taking score, recording the result. Think you can beat me? Think again. In Manly I've seen it behind a rifle sight and on the golf course, at the pool and on the bowls rink. I've learned to recognise it as a kind of everyman homage to an Australian sporting archetype.

Sir Donald Bradman is the alpha national hero. He is the unflinching über-Australian who on his first tour to England recorded the results of every game he played on the two-month ocean crossing, including deck quoits. He won at quoits. He won at everything, and in 1939 entered the South Australian squash championship to keep himself fit. Won that, too. The only test he ever failed was his medical for the army, because his eyesight was well below standard. He did a St John Ambulance course instead. He came out top.

Bradman is the patron saint of a recognisably Australian type of competitor. Implacable and prevailing, he scored nineteen centuries against England, eight of them successive, and this in the days when sportsmen looked less like big healthy kids and more like lean and hungry working men. Bradman is not so much a hero as a superhero: Spiderman, Superman, Bradman. *Bradman Saves Australia*, and during the Depression his brilliant batting did become, for a time, a solitary but shining beacon of hope.

But every country has its superheros, even provincial middle-class England. Spiderman, Superman, Henman.

In the inevitable Marvel two-hander, cashing in on the popularity of both our enemies of evil, Bradmania outdoes Henmania every time, and with runs to spare. The sporting Australian is encouraged to find the inner Bradman, praying he might be in there somewhere. I know only too well where to find my inner Henman, the nervous pecker, too self-effacing and scared of victory ever to be mistaken for his long-lost superhero twin, Cockman.

Which is not necessarily a bad thing. I can't finally be persuaded that Western civilisation depends on crushing Australia's top order, or beating John Mater at golf, or straining to an outright win in the pub to pub. I'm a competitive person, can't deny that, but I'm not as competitive as I sometimes think I am. Or would like to be. I'm not prepared to fight to the death, my own or someone else's, as required by the envied killer instinct. I go only as far as the near-death experience. That's the limit of my will, and the light at the end of the tunnel is the way I came in, my loser's grateful realisation that pushing myself any further simply isn't worth the candle. At which point (which is admittedly quite a long way down the track), if I haven't won already, I retreat towards the light and lose.

By about eleven kilometres I can't distract myself a second longer, but it hardly matters because I'm within imagination of the finish. I reinterpret urgent signs of physical breakdown as ringing endorsements of character. And as I cross the line (sixty-five minutes, *not bad*) what have I actually achieved?

I creak, my timbers shiver. I honestly didn't expect still to be character-building, not at thirty-eight years old, which is getting on a bit for a small boy of my age. I was hoping that these kinds of nasty but allegedly uplifting experiences would come to an end, and then I'd find out what this monumental character, built so optionally and painfully over so long, was for. And, if it existed at all, I thought I'd know by now how much of my built character depended on sport.

I can see what it's for in Billy Kerrigan. Running makes him strong, and keeps him off the booze and thankful to God. It saves him.

Fifth Test

In the absence of other expressions of national identity, sport takes on a special importance. The imperial 'cult' of 'manly' games has become the last redoubt of English national identity in a world that doesn't give a damn about England.

Mike Marqusee, *Anyone but England*, 2005

It comes to us all, sooner or later: sport without actually taking part. For me, for twenty years, Saturday has been match day. I've been on the pitch, so I've never fully committed myself to the experience of watching, either live or on television, but spectating is the taste of fate for ex-players everywhere, their age laid bare by coming 6,549th. In anything.

Since the day I stepped off the plane I've been looking forward to watching the cricket from England, the 2005 Ashes series. I'd hoped to observe local small-of-the-morning reactions to England's predictable submission, but no one else in Manly has seemed that bothered. It's as if in Manly spectating doesn't count as a sporting experience. Also, Australia's English summer of victories takes place every four years in the middle of the night, a routine dream experience and therefore no special need to miss an early night for an early start, home by four on flexitime for a last daylight hour in the surf. Or a set of tennis or half a round of golf. Whatever you fancy: croquet, bicycle racing, life drawing, netball, bookshop browsing, a little light jogging or competitive sixteen-foot skiff sailing. Manly has it all.

I ask Maria, formerly of Portugal and Angola, rifle shooter and marathon runner and pub to pubber, if she follows the cricket.

'Nah, mate, Manly Sea Eagles. Go, Manly, go!'

I'd already been to Manly Oval to see the Marlins, the semi-professional rugby union team, and it was a disaster. I didn't want to watch, I wanted to play, even though recently I've been dreaming matches played in the dark. I can't see the ball and the opposition keep intercepting, which is most dispiriting, even when I'm asleep.

Watching the Manly Marlins hadn't cheered me up, not least because the pies ran out before half-time, the raffle was won by a committee member, and the Marlinettes cheerleaders were pre-teen schoolgirls shaking their pom poms to a song about female orgasm – 'Take Me to a Higher Place'. No one else seemed to notice, as if inside the Manly Oval only sport counts, the song lyrics nothing but an innocent ditty about mountaineering. The game itself was played in front of 500 people, with drowsy shouts of 'C'mon Manly' and a sense that everyone was more familiar with the ref ('George') than with the teams.

This was clearly not the spectating hub of Manly sporting life, and that's because I'd chosen the wrong version of rugby. The real action is at Brookvale Oval, home of NRL rugby league club the Manly Warringah Sea

Eagles. When they're going well, as they are in 2005, the Sea Eagles get 15,000 people in. Maria has a season ticket. This means she gets a complimentary maroon beanie she doesn't want, and which I can pull over my head as an entry-level disguise.

A sunny Sunday afternoon, and Manly need a win to stay in contention for the play-offs. The crowd is over 15,000, but seems bigger because one side and one end of the ground are not seats or terraces, but slopes of short-cropped grass. These are the hills once common in Australian sports grounds, made famous in England by the legend of the Hill at the SCG. This has now been upgraded and renamed Yabba's Hill, after the fan who barracked Douglas Jardine for waving away a fly: 'Jardine! Leave our flies alone!' Later, the Sydney Hill became better known for drunkenness and fighting, and in 1971 the English cricket team left the field after John Snow was pelted by beer cans. The Hill is missed, apparently; it kept the players honest.

At Brookie, Maria always sits halfway up the hill, level with the far twenty-metre line. As we weave through to her usual spot, I see the universal identifiers of a sports crowd, the rolled match programme dibbed in a back pocket, the safety in colour-by-numbers as maroon and white Manly jerseys swarm and settle, but that's OK, because I have my Manly hat. I see men with pages of that day's paper jammed under the bridge of their sunglasses, to protect their noses from sunburn, and as everyone finds a place I listen to the rustle and hum.

The gulping, the chomping, the swallowing. It's about watching, sure, but also eating and drinking, and at Brookie the pies just keep on coming, an obvious benefit of full professionalism. Manly fans bring blankets to sit on, and because there are as many women as men, it feels like a convivial mass picnic. The hill at the northern end is a no-alcohol family zone, where there's a petting zoo and a bouncy-castle cow that never stops wobbling, as if jigging to the music whenever the Manly Under-7s score.

This match between tiny vigorous children is one of several community curtain-raisers, and under the influence of an early beer, I start to regret my youth. At first, this seems a fairly routine consequence of outside drinking on a warm afternoon. Then, with the hill filling up and sunshine fawning over the lush greenness of the pitch, and after another beer, I regret the youth I never had in Australia. Which is plain silly, and reminds me why playing is better than watching – no time for this type of nonsense.

All the same, if I'd grown up in Manly, Australia, I'd be going home to a barbecued tea and a cabinet of medals and trophies. Or more likely, given my reading of the stats from the Australian Bureau of Statistics, I'd be driving my average Australian low-slung ute to a drive-in burger 'n' bottle shop before spending the rest of Sunday slumped in front of televised sport. The only flaw in this statistic, in fact any statistic, is that I haven't met any average Australians. Even *I* could be an average Australian, if my family had paid attention to the posters and the ads in the papers and the steady English pilgrimage to Australia House. Ten pounds! We had our chance, and the sport I'm watching in Manly is the life that could have been mine. In my short-sleeved shirt in winter, my sunglasses, and for purposes of assimilation my Sea Eagles beanie, I spectate an alternative existence, the road not taken.

After the Under -21s, and then the second team match, the amazing Eaglettes come on. These are real cheerleaders, or as real as cheerleaders get, lithe young women that every man in the ground would sleep with, and still be back for kick-off. They're undressed in maroon hot pants and silver tinsel, to my mind a much underused clothing fabric, and they pump their sparkly pom-poms and stomp their silver boots.

I think the obvious: those boots would really cut up a pitch in winter. Then I realise this *is* winter, and again the weather is making the difference. The simplest reason is often the truest one, and this is why Australians excel at sport. Even the stadium depends on the weather, because in Wigan these grass banks would be mudslides, whatever the season. In the Manly winter they're dry and solid and making rugby league a community picnic. Not that Brookvale Oval is parochial. Far from it – the actor Russell Crowe's bodyguard is a man called Spud, a former Sea Eagle, and Spud's wife Monique trains the Manly cheerleaders. We are connected by a direct line to matters of international security.

The match starts and the referee misses something and a man sitting behind me boos viciously. And some more. When the game moves on he turns to his friend. 'What happened?' Not that he doesn't care, it's just that he already deserves a win after the effort he's put in to get here.

Supporters care more about results than players, in inverse proportion to their ability to influence the result. Players know when they've been outplayed, and it's a fair cop. That's sport for you. But to the supporter, it's never fair. The fan puts in as much effort to be there this week as last, perhaps more, and expects these efforts to be reflected on the pitch. Losing is therefore always an injustice, though I don't sense, as Manly concede a soft early try, any imminent danger in the crowd's disappointment.

The scariest sound on the Hill isn't barracking. It's hearing a voice immediately behind me saying, in a fairly unconcerned way, 'Don't vomit, mate.'

They trot out Allan Border at half-time (I shuffle forward and to the side a little), but he's too far away to see and I can't hear what he's saying and no one seems interested in any case. Just another all-time sporting legend. Ho hum. Boy-next-door stuff.

As a visiting Englishman my one big disadvantage, up on the Hill at Brookie, is inexperience. I have no idea how it used to be in the good old days, and regretting the past is among Manly's biggest pleasures. I see that now, and I'm a quick learner, so near the end of the game I'm already feeling nostalgic for the beginning, when my pies and beers were still a treat in front of me.

Manly lose the game in the last thirty seconds, unable to defend their own last-minute comeback score. What did they expect? They were playing against the never-say-die Cowboys from North Queensland, and for me this kind of defeat to Australians is entirely familiar. Though perhaps not in rugby league, where the Cringe is so deeply embedded a last-minute defeat would almost count as a victory.

There are supposedly no unbreakable patterns in sport, but Great Britain's rugby league players haven't won a series against Australia since 1970. Looking for stiffer competition than the north of England, the biggest matches in the world are now Australia against Australia, in the annual State of Origin series that sets New South Wales against Queensland. Australia always wins, but Australian excellence isn't always helpful. In London in

1932, against the English champion Joe Davis, Australian Walter Lindrum won the world billiards title by making a record break of 4,137 points. At a maximum of three points a shot. The break contained 1,295 cannons, making Lindrum so expert and the match so boring he killed billiards as an international sporting spectacle.

Maybe rugby league doesn't need international rivalries, because the Sea Eagles and Cowboys dinged and donged and there wasn't too long a queue at the beer caravan, and with a beer and a pie in the sunshine what more could anyone want? That was the question I asked myself during the first quarter. The answer came to me at the start of the second: another beer and another pie. And so on. This is my revenge as a spectator. For years I've been selfless, taking exercise, keeping fit, reducing the burden on the NHS. For which I've had no thanks or refunds on my income tax, an omission the government may soon have cause to regret.

In NRL folklore, every Australian has two favourite teams: their own, and whoever's playing Manly. Not me. One game and I'm hooked: a Manly Warringah Sea Eagles fan for life. Or at least I thought so, but that was before I understood that for the spectator every match is a gamble. At the cinema, you have a fair idea of what you're paying to see. At Brookvale Oval, you're in the mood for something light with a happy ending, and often as not you get *Titanic*.

Or the other way round, but when it turns out well you can't go back for the rerun. You were either there or you weren't, so the paying spectators share the privilege of being alive and involved in the here and now, though without the pain of actually taking the field. That's a sound return on a A$20 ticket, especially with nobody checking at the gates for knowledge, insight or even patience. I expect every player I see on the pitch to be fit and fearless, because I'm in the business of supporting, not empathising, and all I need to bring with me is certainty. Who should play where and why. It was better in the old days. I'd have scored that myself, with my eyes closed. My *grandma* could have scored that, and she's been dead ten years. The ref's a tosser.

And because every other supporter feels much the same way, it's like being back on a team, with all the comfort that can bring. I'm taking part, I'm involved. I'm welcome.

By my third home match in a row, I'm beginning to see the difference between bad sport and bad theatre. Watching your own team is like being the mother of at least one if not more of the actors. The performance can and occasionally will be awful, truly dreadful, but it always holds your attention. It's unwatchable, compelling, as the cycle of life exemplified by a sports club makes its yearly seasonal turn: struggle, defeat, hope springing eternal.

For the England cricket fan, hope did not spring eternal. It came to an end at about the end of the twentieth century. I'd have liked to cheer on England as I cheered on Manly, wearing the colours in a big open stadium with live attractions and a bouncy inflatable cow. It didn't seem a lot to ask.

I therefore bought a ticket to the second stage of the 1999 Cricket World Cup, the Super Six round. The semi-finals seemed overly optimistic even then, but by the Super Six Bangladesh and Holland would be flying home and the serious cricket could begin.

England failed to reach the Super Six, in a home World Cup. I ended up gormless at the Oval, me and my friend James watching Australia play India, sitting between a man who fed us sweet Indian cakes and a giggling Australian barman. He'd been given the ticket and a day off by his English boss, who preferred to stay at work.

There were consolations – we'd get to see Tendulkar in his pomp. McGrath had him third ball. England weren't even playing, but an Australian fast bowler had ruined my day before lunch. Paul Reiffel then downed a pigeon with a throw from third man, and a supporter up from Devon, who was also missing England but not his day off, yelled 'Burrrd-kullerrrr!' every time Reiffel touched the ball, which wasn't often because India didn't manage much of a total.

In Manly, six years later, I now had the big decision of where to watch England fail to win back the Ashes. For anyone with no eye for a ball who can't get to a stadium or afford a ticket, the community values of sport are usually accessible in a bar. This is as true in Australia as it is in England, and in Australia there's no shortage of choice because bars and sports clubs are everywhere.

I therefore go back to the Manly Fishing and Sporting Association one weekend afternoon to check it over as a place to watch the cricket. Bobby Yonks is in the same seat as last time, and I could have sworn his mates are as well, though this time the serious Fishos drinkers are involved in a competitive Fishos sport. With the rugby league on a giant screen in the background (Manly getting thumped at Cronulla), the Fishos are locked in a trivia quiz.

Before I know it, I'm sunk in the cinema squab of afternoon drinking and cigarette smoke, abetted by an unnecessary PA that finds out the pathos of empty space as surely as at a dubious wedding. The quiz is very slow. Rather than questions, the amplified MC might be offering us a selection of topics for conversation. In this way, in the long gap between one question and the next, we discuss whether Buenos Aires is further south than Montevideo, and why so many countries (six) end in the letter Y, and whether any place in Australia is more than a thousand kilometres from the sea in every direction.

To be useful in a trivia team there's no point knowing what everyone else knows, like the best-selling Australian recording artist of the 1980s. No idea, but I'm one hundred per cent certain I know who was married to Anne Hathaway. I clinch it on question twenty-five by recognising Picasso in a photograph, though everyone else wants it to be the weatherman on Channel 9, and then a rough-trade lesbian from a rival table bets a jug of Carlton Black that it's not fucking Pick-Arsehole anyone, matey-pies, and question number twenty-six – Would it be possible to watch the Ashes at the Manly Fishos club? – doesn't even spark a discussion because the answer is definitively no.

By the second session I'd be so drunk Anne Hathaway would be a country ending in Y to the south of a thousand kilometres.

This is a shame. I'd have liked to watch the cricket in a club, because when you don't belong a sense of belonging is that much more important. This helps explain why Australia has so much sport. A club is a conscious decision to organise an activity on a more permanent and continuing basis, and that activity is usually drinking. The club also offers a source of mutual support and new friendships. It becomes the extended family most immigrants leave behind, so no wonder the club culture established itself so convincingly in the suburbs of Sydney. With the clubs came sports, as a cheap and easy-to-organise form of entertainment. Sports clubs now exist for every age and temperament, and not joining in must be like snubbing your family, thinking you can manage without them.

Stumbling home, chuffed with another victory on Australian soil, I recognise that from the Fishos to the golf course I've been taking advantage of the attested Sydney talent for making people welcome. Or as Manly Golf Club president Gerry Elkan likes to put it, 'In Sydney you're innocent until proven guilty; in Melbourne you're guilty until proven innocent.' I'm drunk enough to see that Gerry, if he stopped to punctuate, would speak in semi-colons.

He also reminds me of the second reason I'm hesitant about watching the Ashes in a club. The locals might find me out – guilty. Guilty of taking English cricket too seriously. I therefore decide to watch it in the pub, where among strangers the consequences of *England Collapse* are potentially less embarrassing.

The Steyne Hotel is a two-storey building on the ocean corner of the Corso. It looks like a turreted castle with an 'elaborate range of brickwork in the Art Deco style', as described by the Manly council planning committee when they reject applications to neonise this 'Item of Environmental Heritage'. The Steyne has a roof bar, a walk-in ground-floor bar, and nine other bars in between, though when it opened in 1860 it was advertised 'as near as practicable, to resemble . . . an English Hotel'. It closed within three months, and reopened under new management. Rebuilt in 1935 (hence the Art Deco), it is now patently Australian, a rambling emporium for drinking with a reputation for late-night fighting. I've heard it called the Bloodhouse, but that was in the library, and maybe doesn't count.

More certain is the pub's active role in Manly's sporting history. It was at the Steyne Hotel in 1903 that a committee first met officially to set up the golf club. The Steyne was where Manly residents conceived the original petition for the bowls club, and the provisional rules for the lifesaving club. It was also used for Roman Catholic mass, illegal gambling and coroner's inquests after drownings, making it as good a place as any to despair at the lifeless corpse of English cricket.

It is now seven p.m., half an hour before the first ball of the first Ashes Test of 2005. The time difference fits the cricket perfectly into a standard Manly schedule, the first session slotting in at early-evening prime time, a little taster from Lord's to see Australia start strongly. Once the youngsters have been adequately inspired, or reassured, they can be tucked up in bed by ten.

When it's the other way round and England play in Australia, if you're paying attention from England the first session begins at 2.30 in the morning. This time is fixed in law after a campaign sponsored by Esther Rantzen to protect children from trauma, and it means that for true English cricket fanatics the suffering is aggravated by sleep deprivation. For the rest of us, the mystery of the first day's play is revealed on morning radio with the words: 'Bad news from the Gabba.' Or in November 2002, Aggers ruining my morning, my Christmas, my winter, with his memorable first words from that year's series: 'We feared it might be bad. No one expected it would be *this* bad.'

At the corner of the Steyne Hotel, ground floor, the sign for Harry's Sports Bar is picked out in green and gold, and as I push open the door I feel I'm finally competing on a level playing field. In bars, the standard explanations for Australian superiority no longer apply: the favourable climate, the superior diet, better sporting facilities. I and other regulars should be able to have a decent and evenly matched argument about why England–Australia matters. Which of course I'll be aiming to win.

That's not how it happens. After months of waiting and a summer of raised expectations, and no Ashes victory at Lords since 1934, I take a seat at the empty counter and watch England lose the toss. So far so recognisable. Within fifteen overs Australia are 66 for 3, and the world as I know it is tilting. Nobody in the Steyne Hotel except me is excited. Or even very obviously interested. Harry's Sports Bar is next to the TAB, the Australian state bookies, and most of the punters, all men, are more interested in the TV showing race eight from Geelong. The third TV in the row has greyhounds, and an Asian-looking man keeps rushing in and out with last-minute bets on the dogs.

I buy beer and assume that Australians with a passion for cricket will be flooding into the bar any minute now, after their tea perhaps, or when the children are safely in bed, but Harry's Sports Bar remains as empty as it was for the first ball of the series. In stormed Harmison, off the long run. Down went the ball. Nothing happened. Fantastic cricket. Second ball, and here comes Harmison again, and down goes the ball and Australian batsman Langer is injured and play stops indefinitely. Just why is it that foreigners can't understand that cricket's an unbeat-able game?

No apparent interest from the Manly locals, either. On the bright side, this means no choruses of the deadly 'Aussie Aussie Aussie, oi oi oi'. I take an amble, carrying my schooner, through the rest of the Steyne. It's huge, and several televisions in several bars are showing the match as background, without commentary. The truth is, in the oldest and sportiest pub in Manly, there are no obvious followers of Australia against England at cricket.

Mind you, 97 for 5 at lunch. Ho ho. As I can't find anyone Australian eager to share the moment, I go home and watch the next session sitting alone on my sofa, this time with the sound turned up.

I don't know what to expect. Several people had already suggested to me that Australians are good at sport because their television is rubbish. This makes going to bed at nine for five a.m. training less of a sacrifice, and before now I'd spent an hour or two checking if this could be right. Flicking between the channels, I'd discovered that at any moment of the day you can see a seventeen-year-old Australian girl breaking a swimming record. I'd also caught snatches of netball, rugby league, Australian Rules, football, live Tour de France, athletics, and a documentary about Swiss Alpine wrestling. It was as if there was only sport, and no TV on television at all. I once watched the end of a bowls match in which an Australian pair beat an English pair so quickly it upset the schedule for the rest of the evening.

There had to be more to Australian television than this, and there was. They have a channel where *Neighbours* alternates with random episodes of *Dr Who*, and *Neighbours* was in celebration mode with a plot line featuring a twenty-year reunion. I used to watch *Neighbours* as a student, about twenty years ago, and it was thoughtful of them to have put this on just for me. They even found Plain Jane Superbrain, who'd travelled back to Ramsey Street from the UK, where for twenty years she'd been living as my cosseted fantasy mistress. Fictional characters have such varied lives.

When *Neighbours* moved to a break, on national TV in winter, I saw my first ever television commercial for cricket. There was nothing showy about it.

Like fun? Play cricket.
playcricket.com

What could be simpler, what could be *more true*? No need for the chairman of Tesco to advise at great expense on marketing – simply tell it as it is. Of course, I thought, this is why the Australians are going to win the Ashes. They don't mess about.

Australian cricket and television have history. It was television income that moved Kerry Packer to split the game in the late 1970s with his World Series Cricket. The TV spectacle was so central to Packer's strategy that he paid people to attend the matches, ensuring the 'live' atmosphere his TV viewers and advertisers demanded. This was an idea ahead of its time but in those days, along with floodlights and coloured jerseys, it was used to illustrate the mainly English fear that Packer would 'Americanise' the good old Empire game of cricket. In fact he Australianised the game, filling it with attack and character.

At that time, as far as I was concerned, Packer's World Series Cricket was brilliant. It weakened the Australian cricket team. Over we went for the Ashes in 1978/9, and the Australians, without their stars, were roundly trounced by an England team captained by Mike Brearley. Even better, Brearley was quiet, reserved, an archetypal English-man in every sense, including being useless at cricket.

In 2005, the Ashes are on satellite Foxtel *and* terrestrial SBS. This is because since 1992 free-to-air channels have first option on forty-one Australian sporting events, including every rugby and cricket international both home and away (in England, there are nine events protected for terrestrial broadcast). The accessibility of international sport surely helps quicken the pulse of Australian youngsters, even in a country with a TV culture that can stuff three commercial breaks into an episode of *The Simpsons*. During the Tri-Nations rugby matches (free-to-air) they break for adverts at injuries, so you never know who hit who.

At the first-day lunch break, the SBS studio pundits are former Test players Dean Jones and Greg Matthews, recognisable but wider and grey-haired, like those faces from *Neighbours* twenty years on. This comes as a welcome shock: Australian cricketers grow old. We see, far more often than we should, what an old bore a former hero like Bob Willis can become. Australians on the other hand, forever fixed in their prime, are able and athletic without end. Allan Border is never a day older than the last time he gutsed it out against England, on standby at the Brookvale Oval even now, ready to strap on the pads whenever Australia need him.

Greg and Dean look unlikely first Test replacements, but the battling spirit lives on. They're predicting an immediate Australian fightback, no matter the freak figures of the first session. As the picture blinks back to Lord's, the old ground looks spectacular, England from a distance like earth from space, green and blue, much more beautiful than it is.

Along with the Channel 4 pictures, it turns out that SBS is broadcasting the Channel 4 commentary, and here comes Richie, an Australian voice forever summer in England. Richie Benaud was always a significant presence. Not only was he responsible for the worst impressions in Britain (*everyone* thinks they can do a Richie), the silver fox evolved a new category of Cringe, the Commentary Cringe. He made Peter West and Tom Graveney look like amateur duffers, dirt-trackers. He was so good that for a long time I never knew he was once a successful Australian cricket captain. In provincial English living rooms he was simply an essential fixture of the cricket season, and the reason we lost the commentary Ashes every time – a burnt microphone that resides for ever on the Benaud mantelpiece. Today's commentators can compete for it, but they'll never get to take it home.

My favourite among the Poms is Geoffrey Boycott, who between his playing and commentating days went to Bangkok at his own expense for a borderline-legal personality transplant. The dreary, infuriating batsman who blocked for a draw in one-day internationals reappeared as an incisive thinker with straight but tempered opinions, a flashing turn of phrase and instinctive flair in his use of colloquialisms.

Unfortunately, Channel 4 also employs Michael Atherton, living proof that this process of enlightened personality change is far from automatic. As a batsman, Atherton used to consider every shot in the book, and then play defensively. As a commentator, he gives the impression he's deciding between all manner of Benaudian possibilities, then offers us the cliché. In fact he ponders an impressive range of clichés, many of which he's practised against a machine, and makes sure he uses the one which sounds most familiar. It is the classic approach, the textbook straight bat.

I can't forgive Atherton for ruining the 90s, for losing us a decade. Atherton was the fixed hinge in the revolving-door selection policy of that dimmest period in English cricket. Everyone was picked. Even I could have been picked, but only for one game, no matter how well or badly I played. The only certainty was Atherton, standing at slip radiating negativity, chin in one hand, the other playing with the dirt he's going to deny he has in his pocket, incapable of offering his players any gesture or sense or spark of verve or even hope. Another humiliation and there's Atherton, keeping his job as captain, avoiding the blame. Now he sits in the commentary box making suggestions, when if he had anything useful to offer he should have said so at the time, as the captain in the middle. Richie did.

As a player Atherton embodied the Cringe. Against Australia his record says it all: Series Played 7, Series Lost 7. In his final Test innings he was out for an irrelevant nine in an England follow-on, tamely submitting to Glenn McGrath for an abject nineteenth time. In my Cringe-addled mind, Atherton has forfeited his existence as a human being, reduced to a kind of skilled but irrevocably evil puppet who blights the post-match presentations. (No, Freddie! Don't get too close! He'll suck out your soul!) He is the force of darkness who made a generation of England cricket fans lose the will to live.

From the moment I hear Atherton's voice, the tilt of phrases shaping to be interesting and then always managing to duck, I know we're doomed.

We lose the first Test by 239 runs.

* * *

Another Test match, another day. Sitting on my Australian sofa swearing at Michael Atherton isn't going to shift the Cringe. I should be out there in Manly, doing my bit to help, preferably somewhere with the sound turned down. But what contribution, exactly, can I hope to make?

My brother Tim, while researching his Ph.D. on French literature, claimed not to have missed a single televised ball of a home Test in three years. This is one reason I regret not continuing my studies. Another is that if I had, I could more easily understand the many useful discoveries of sociology. In particular, instead of seeing sports betting as an invention of the devil and a criminal waste of time and money, I'd understand that 'by stimulating suspense and uncertainty, betting satisfies important emotional needs for people who find their lives becoming more and more predictable'.

Nothing in life has come to seem so predictable as an Ashes defeat. Contesting the Cringe, I could always try to match the Australians at the bookies. Put a few dollars on. Get involved. Travel to the sporting dark side where athletes live and breathe on behalf of the punter, their fates conjoined by money risked on the outcome.

The Australians are champion gamblers. A population of twenty million spends £37 billion on bets, whereas Britain with a population nearly three times the size manages only £5 billion more. That's pathetic. It's as if we're not even trying, and it's said that Labour sports minister Richard Caborn was so shocked by what he saw in Australia that he modified his plans to deregulate casinos. Typical. He's probably set back our efforts to catch them up by years.

In Australia, it's no worries, because safety procedures are openly in place. They come in the form of a no-nonsense statement from the government: 'If you can't afford to bet and lose, don't bet.'

But how else would it be exciting? Though falling behind as a nation, Britain can still boast some fine individual contenders. The footballer Michael Owen is reported to have wagered away £2 million, though he admits only to loose change, say 40,000 quid. According to the Australian government, Owen doesn't have a problem: he can afford to lose it.

The Australians, of course, have heroic punters of their own, like the Packer dynasty. In Australian mythology Kerry's Granddad Robert found a ten-shilling note in the street, and bet his way from Tasmania to Sydney to get a start in newspapers. This may even be true, because the gold rush of the early 1850s confirmed the notion that anyone in Australia could strike it lucky. Ever since, it's been a gamble to move to Australia, for whatever reason, and if Australians weren't willing to take a chance they'd still be in Zagreb or Da Nang, or Minchinhampton. Betting on footie matches or dogs or poker machines is just a sedentary version of heading for the hills, hoping to strike it rich without the bother of a donkey.

Gambling also appeals in Australia because of its evident egalitarianism – everyone is equally lucky. Only they're not. If you lose you're a loser. If you win, you're a lord of the universe with a divine backhander that promises all-areas access to the ravelled connections behind the mysterious workings of chance. Basically, everyone wants to be a lucky bastard.

For a passive activity that requires no physical aptitude, gambling is curiously macho. At the golf club John Maclean, who's seventy-six, happily had a flutter on our four-ball matches and also liked a wager at bridge.

'Of course there's no money on the table when ladies are involved.'

It hardly needs be said: the risk measures the man. And in the tempting of fate, unbowed bravado is traditionally the manliest approach. There's a story about Kerry Packer in a casino with a fellow punter who won't stop bragging about how well off he is. Packer eventually cracks and asks the man how much he's worth, and with his chest puffed up the man lists the zeds and the boggling noughts.

'Toss you for it,' Packer says.

To win back the Ashes, we need some Packer swagger: stand up, be counted. After the humiliation of the first Test, I refuse to surrender to the national habit, which at this point requires lying down and dying like an Atherton cricket team.

Defiantly, I stride to the Steyne Hotel Bloodhouse on the eve of the second Test and this time, instead of going straight to Harry's Sports Bar, I stop in at the small connecting annexe which is the TAB and bottle shop. Any fool can tell it's a TAB because there's a huge poster on the door in the style of a Sex Pistols album cover: 'God Save the Queen (Because Nothing Can Save the Poms)'.

The TAB at the Steyne is a window in an off-licence. There's a carpet beneath my feet, a counter under my elbow, but Las Vegas it isn't. An indulgent uncle of a man, with a round face and a beard, gives me a printout of odds on the cricket. One dollar on Australia to win the second Test gets me back one dollar sixty cents. One dollar on England pays five dollars twenty. Money talks, and the betting exchange is where the smart money chats to relax, as opposed to the Formula 1 paddock, say, where the more stupid money shouts its mouth off. The smart money reckons England are doomed, the dollars and cents as scornful in their way as Australia's *Daily Telegraph* on England's capitulation at Lord's: 'We saw the march of the lemmings, as five batsmen threw themselves off the cliff as if their end had been preordained, built into them as a species.'

Not just another country, but a divergent species, *Loserus Anglicanus*. Meanwhile the Australian species is itself moving on, and in Manly Mike Taylor and his surfing pals are down on the beach turning hard-skinned and scaly, agile, recuperative. They're evolving into amphibian lizards, with a ferocious eye for a ball.

But then last time, during the Lord's Test, I'd done nothing to help England out. Must try harder.

The talking money tells me that Australia is the rational bet. No worries, mate. In fact, any fool can see that betting on Australia in cricket is a win–win situation. If Australia win, I'm rich (and a lord of the universe who's unravelled the secret mysteries of the etcetera). If England win, I've wasted my money and I'm mortal as plumber's putty, but who cares? England have won.

My sporting judgement is also at stake. The week before the Lord's Test, Adam Gilchrist the all-rounder (batsman/reptile/wicketkeeper) smashed a century in the final one-day international. This does not bode well for England. The form book isn't any more encouraging. In 2002/3 England lost the first Ashes Test. They surrendered as meekly in the second. The same thing happened in 2001, and also 1999 – lose one Test, lose another. The smart money shrugs, pouts; listen to the money. But wait – in 1997 England *won* the first Test. And the second? All out in the first innings for 77. Like gravity, the Cringe reasserts itself, and the smart bet is to back the strong, because the meek will not inherit the earth.

I can't do it. Despite the fact that we haven't won for eighteen years, and Australia have just come good in the Lord's Test, and Michael Atherton's negative energy will be at Trent Bridge seeping down from the commentary box for all five days, I physically can't tick the box on the piece of paper which means I'm reading the stars as an Australia win.

The avuncular man in the TAB leans forward with one hand supporting his chin and the other playing piano on the counter. I impulsively decide that the trick is to make big, occasional bets. Write books; get married; have kids. Treat England–Australia like any other vital life-decision, and bet against all common sense on the outcome most devoutly to be wished. Then, instead of instant gratification, life and five-day cricket will begin its extended Chinese torture: you may have been right, you may have been wrong.

It's about quarter past seven, fifteen minutes before the start of the second Test. It's dark outside. I fill in my slip for England, and tick the A$200 box. To convert dollars into pounds, halve the amount and then take a bit more off. The vagueness of this calculation explains why I've never watched cricket from a corporate box, but in any case A$200 is not peanuts and although the man in the TAB has seen it all before, every type of desperate longing, he raises his eyebrows and checks that I really mean it. Two hundred dollars. On England. I gulp, recognised in betting shops worldwide as an affirmative.

He then shows me how to feed the ticket into a machine; the machine doesn't think too hard about it, and gives me back a receipt. The money itself I have to hand to the man, as if despite its apparent docility, the computer can't actually be trusted. On the bottom of my receipt, on the bottom of every TAB receipt printed that day in Australia, even for the dogs at Capalaba, it says: 'Can Anyone Save the Poms this Time?'

Yes. I can. I've linked my fate to theirs, invested my money. They *owe* me. Not just for the A$200 but the blind faith, and nearly two decades of unbroken frustration. It was cricket that first got us into the Cringe, so cricket will get us out again – it's about time I and England beat Australia together.

This is how gambling invades the mind. It's a cosmic deal, my identity involved as a side bet. If I win, I'm a winner. I go next door to Harry's Sports Bar and take a seat at the counter to watch the first few overs. Or as much as I can take, whichever lasts longer. I settle in, a newly initiated member of the TAB brotherhood that includes me and the Asian man on the dogs, and a couple of painter-decorators pissed off with the horses. I am instantly a possible god and a serious waster, here with the stale carpet and the obligatory Irishman telling no one special he ate a slice of ham for his tea.

Strauss is batting and Warne drops a catch. It's as if Shane is putting the money in my pocket (more than a thousand dollars!), and I wonder if the money changes the way I'm watching. Betting is an excuse to be interested, and livens up dull events like horses running round a field. But sitting in the bar drinking VB and following the cricket, I'm interested anyway. The gambling is a drug I don't need.

Which is how it always starts, and doesn't mean I couldn't become addicted. I like the idea of other people doing my work for me, especially as I have the will to win but not the skill or the temperament. It would seem, if I want to beat the Australians, that I do need representing after all. So I take my will to win and will England on, because that's what I always do. At the same time I stand to win about a week's wages, to *earn* it, and it's good to see Vaughan and Flintoff working hard for me. They respect the question I've asked of fate; they support my courting of fortune.

As a route to success, betting is the opposite of training and application, those modern sporting virtues. It's an amateur mystery, the gleeful knowledge everyone has that with the right luck anything is possible, anything at all. In an Australian TAB you can probably place a bet on it.

Second Test, third day
In the second innings England are 84 for 6, like night-time, floods, winter, any of nature's regular calamities. I watch England lose my money. Don't they *care*? The Cringe smugly reasserts itself, an invitation for all England to catastrophise: we will never win at any sport against Australia ever again no matter how long I may live.

I regret the bets I didn't make. Rational bets like England losing in three days, on rain, on Flintoff popping his shoulder just when we need him, on our best player not being an Englishman, on our captain unable to score a run, on *England Collapse*. It is another slow death, or would be, if it wasn't so quick. But then a debatable charm of cricket is that even quick deaths seem slow.

Second Test, fourth day
It's funny how a bet changes size. Yesterday, with England in trouble, A$200 was a huge amount of money and far more than I could sensibly afford. I was a jangling fool to

have risked it on the England cricket team, species-bred for uselessness. *Loserus Anglicanus*. *Loose anus* for short, especially in a nervous run-chase.

When I wake up the next morning, England have dreamed Australia to a woeful 175 for 8, and A$200 is a pitiful amount of money. The English cricketers are national heroes of bulldog character making Australians seem brittle and flaky, like snakeskins empty of their inner reptile.

This is the magical elastic territory of If Only, where gambling roams free.

England need only two wickets on the fourth day to win, and there is no better feeling in Australia than strolling along the Manly promenade, moonlight on the breakers, heading for the early-evening Bloodhouse where England will complete their victory in the second Test. Our victory. It seems I can predict the future, and this is a skill that will surely come in handy. More immediately, I shall watch Australia fail to make the hundred runs they need and then I shall collect my winnings, not just the money, but the side bet on my character. *I am a winner.*

Every screen in Harry's Sports Bar is replaying the Sea Eagles one-point victory in their latest bid for the play-offs. I go through to a back bar, where a small TV above an arcade golf game is the only television in the entire Steyne Hotel showing the cricket. As Australia refuse to be bowled out, chipping away at the runs, other televisions mysteriously change over, then all the televisions, and then a big screen descends from the ceiling, at both ends of the bar. In every bar. The locals gather and start chuckling and retelling jokes from the papers, as if covertly they've been paying attention all the time.

'What do Geraint Jones and Michael Jackson have in common?'

'No one knows why they wear gloves.'

I am isolated and idiotic, with my head in my hands. I don't know where to look, and each ball I rotate to a different screen hoping one among so many will bring us luck. The English players have no idea of the suffering they're causing, and when Australia need ten runs to win Steve Harmison bowls four wides and I involuntarily pick up the bar stool I've been chewing and I'm going to . . . what? What exactly am I going to do?

I was going to throw it at a big-screen image of Harmison, or personally smash the continent of Australia. I close my eyes – I'm having a near-death experience, and I need to turn round and quietly get back out the way I came in. I open my eyes and gently put the stool down, but something has changed, or come to an end. I've finally had enough.

The Cringe has finished me, and by the time Australia need a mere four runs to win I am a broken man. The evidence is in the chest area, a strain, the overburdened muscles of a heart too often tested. Lee hits Harmison to the boundary. That's it – my heart pulls, strains, breaks. There's a fielder out there. Only three runs to win. We then get the last wicket, I notice, and win the match by two runs. But for a moment I can't move, can't pretend the breaking hasn't happened. The crack is there. I was already conceding, chucking it all in.

And then I'm running round the bar with my hands in fists beside my head, doubling up, hyper ventilating, pushing my cracked apart ribcage back together with my bare hands, patching up my poor abused English cricketing heart.

When I eventually get home I have to take medication. I squint hard at the instructions on the side of the packet.

Paracatemol, take after meals or far too much lager. Yes, I'd remembered it correctly. Important to take precautions for the morning, now that I can predict the future. I have my seat with the gods, and I foresee a headache.

Third Test, first day
The small booth in the bottle shop annexed to the pub is now my lucky TAB. This is where I choose to commune with the gods, and this week my ticket says 'Is Gambling A Problem For You?' It's nice that they care.

Because of England's Ashes history and Geraint Jones, after placing my bet I'll need a drink to calm my nerves. This means that if gambling does become a problem, I'll also have a drink problem.

I did wonder for a matter of oh, seconds, whether I should risk more of my money after influencing the outcome of the second Test. To back England again would be madness, of course it would, but gambling isn't needy like that: it doesn't crave being seen as reasonable. Also, if I don't back England and they lose, I'll blame myself. It's so English to flinch after a victory, and as the sign on the first tee at Warringah public golf course says, 'Winners Don't Quit and Quitters Don't Win.'

Remember, also, that *If It's To Be, It's Up To Me!*

Anything less than A$200 would show a draining of the faith. The odds on England for the third Test are unchanged, because the smart money is far too clever to be deceived by one unlikely victory. So A$200 on England, plus something extra to keep me and the England team moving forwards. Fifty dollars on Vaughan for highest score of the match, because he's been hopeless so far, and I like Vaughan. He sometimes drops easy catches, like I do, and as a captain he's not Michael Atherton.

So on the money goes, A$200 on England and A$50 on the England captain, betting like someone determined not to win, eager to suffer at the altar of English sport. It's as if losing is the only English result I'll recognise.

This time, while handing over my dollars, I have a chat with the bearded old bloke behind the counter. I fantasise that I have his respect, as a punter so clearly in tune with the divine wallpaper. We agree that cricket's a funny old game. He gives me back my receipts on England and Vaughan, and I see quite clearly that he pities me. I have a betting problem, and that problem is that I'm a serial better on England.

I go into the bar, nearly empty again, and sit on my lucky stool and drink my lucky drink. Beer. Vaughan wins the toss, and I kick myself for not betting he'd do that. Then I could have relaxed. Except I can't, because England are batting and this is agony, as bad as if it were me walking out to the middle, repeatedly swallowing my own heart to stop it thumping out of my mouth. The fact is, it's much more exciting watching England bat than bowl. It's so much quicker, usually, but also every ball we stay in is interesting, and a triumph. Every ball *they* stay in is rather dull, and only to be expected. When Australia score runs, it's predictable and dispiriting. Whenever we score, it's a joy and a wonder, every time.

England are scoring runs and haven't lost any wickets. This means that someone will soon be out. Aaaaagh! Vaughan is now coming down the steps, rehearsing his straight bat on the way to the middle. 'It's a big, big moment for the skipper,' Atherton says, stating the bleeding obvious. I can't bear to watch. I leave. I come back when England are 163 for 1. I watch three balls. 163 for 2.

I wake up in the morning and Vaughan has hit a strapping 166, all by himself. I am the chosen one.

Third Test, fifth day

This is almost fun. The Australians narrowly avoid the follow-on, England bat without collapsing, and as Australia attempt to survive the final day, every screen in the Steyne Hotel auto-tunes to rugby league. I eventually find the cricket in their 'Irish' bar, on a TV squeezed between reruns of the Sea Eagles and *Big Brother Australia*. A girl is sitting in the *Big Brother* chair wearing a large-print T-shirt saying *Boys Lie*.

Why yes, Vesna, ain't that the truth.

Cricket being as changeable as it is, by the time I go to bed I'm miserable. It looks unlikely that England are going to win. Worse, Ricky Ponting is saving Australia single-handed, and he's well-set to pass Vaughan's 166. Entrusting my mood so completely to others turns out to be a reliable source of stress, and the money just serves to bring this into focus.

It's even more frustrating, when I wake up the next day, to find out that the ending of the third Test makes no clear separation between good and evil, right and wrong. The match is a draw the Australians have won. Perhaps. Cricket is the only sport supple enough to do this: ask the public to buy a ticket for an all-action thriller, deliver on that promise for four days, then on the fifth turn ambiguous and arty. I lose my A$200 on England, but win A$800 on Vaughan.

* * *

Fourth Test, first day

Seven fifteen p.m. and the Thursday start of another Test match and *another* A$200 on England. No giving ground now, especially as the notion of sensible betting seems thick. It misunderstands the contract, the process, which insists the longer I bet, the more likely I am to lose. On the other hand, what would happen to England without me? What would have happened to Michael Vaughan?

So I put the usual A$200 on England, and also the A$50 on Vaughan, to show my continued support. I also risk A$50 on Steve Harmison for the most wickets, because Harmy is looking glum.

We win the toss, and I can't say I'm surprised.

That was me, too, because since I'd become aware of my ability to commune with the gods, it had seemed a shame to waste the opportunity. I'd therefore spent my time between the third and fourth Tests recruiting divine assistance.

First stop, St Patrick's Estate on the hill of North Head. Built in 1889, the main building is the most striking landmark in Manly, columned and squarely imposing and sand-coloured. It was once Australia's biggest seminary, a training college for Catholic priests, and the splendid central tower is the last structure on Manly's ocean coast to catch the sunset from Sydney and the west of beyond at the end of every day.

Look up, it seems to be saying, *reflect*.

At least that's what it said until 1995, when the building stopped educating clerics and became instead the International School of Management. The Australian flag now flies from the tower – a victory for Australian secularism.

If sport really is a new religion, Australia is ideally placed: it's so little in thrall to the old one. With God on indefinite leave from St Patrick's, but with Vaughan's A$800 solid in my pocket as evidence of visionary insight, I decide to try out St Matthew's Anglican Church on the Corso. It is eight o'clock on a Sunday morning and the vicar is wearing his team kit, a white robe and purple stole and dog collar. He also has a name badge, just in case. In true Anglican tradition the microphones are on the blink, but the moral of the sermon I hear quite clearly: 'If you like Jesus, go and surf.'

I therefore follow the Anglican vicar's advice, and meet beaming Nic Gilmour and his Christian Surfers on the beach, the six of us in wetsuits in a circle, offering thanks for what we're about to receive. And then we're off. I'm on my own for most of the next hour, as with the peace and understanding of God the Christian Surfers catch waves and without it I eat foam and get swept down the beach towards the sewer outlet. Luckily, Nic comes to save me, and not necessarily in the biblical sense.

The Christian Surfers are like a supercharged version of any other sports club. Back in their clubhouse, Nic Gilmour's front room on the road across from the beach, they welcome me in with hot Milo and biscuits and surf videos, Jack Johnson playing over awesome breaking waves in Maui. They don't hide behind back-slapping and knee-strapping and jokes about nurses inspecting testicles. They'll say they love you straight out. It takes a bit of getting used to, especially when all I want is some advice on getting God on England's side in the cricket.

'When you meet the Man at the pearly gates,' Nic asks me, deciding to ignore my question, 'what are you going to say?'

I think for a minute. 'I ran under seventy-five minutes in the City2Surf.'

'Come on, mate, be serious.'

'Can we win the Ashes?'

I suddenly realise what the vicar must have said at the end of his sermon. Not surf, you dolt. If you love Jesus, go and *serve*. I therefore give the winnings from Vaughan's 166 to Nic Gilmour. This is because if I give the money to Christian Surfers Australia, God is more likely to engineer a miraculous win for England in the fourth Test.

'Give us a T-shirt,' I say, uncomfortable with the concept of something for nothing. But the Christian Surfers don't do merchandising, not in the conventional sense. I can have the T-shirt if I listen to Nic's chat, and I pass this news on in gratitude for God's help in the cricket. It's a two-point plan.

1. Everlasting life is a free gift.
2. Who wouldn't be full of joy and forgiveness and be nice to other people?

That's it.

Divinely insured, at least as far as is possible, I feel quietly confident in Harry's Sports Bar as England construct a steady first innings. I even seem to have gained a kind of all-seeing eye, able to watch more than one thing at once, the cricket *and* the swayings of a prowling middle-aged drunk.

'I'M A KIWI!' he shouts. He's talking to the Czech barmaid, loudly but not unkindly, as if allowing for the possibility that she might be hard of hearing. 'BUT I'M OVER HERE HELPING THE AUSTRALIANS OUT!'

He makes a point of talking very loudly to anyone who'll listen. I know that soon he'll be talking very loudly to me.

'THE AUSTRALIANS ARE THE BEST SPORTSMEN IN THE WORLD!'

'How do we know that then?' I ask politely, as Vaughan pads up to Warne.

'JUST ASK THEM!'

Fourth Test, fourth day

They say gambling corrupts, but drinking in an all-male bar at midnight on the Sabbath getting money for other people's labour, I can't see the problem. As the Sunday night of the fourth Test slurs into Monday, I realise through a haze of self-satisfaction and Victoria Bitter that betting makes my heroes into horses. If Trescothick was to pop a hamstring, I wouldn't much mind if he was humanely dispatched at the crease (off the wicket to avoid Warne pitching in the bloodstains). No, that wouldn't bother me at all, not if my money was on Strauss.

Australia are following on and England need to bowl them out quickly to have a manageable winning target. I watch the session as long as I can, but we have a chronic inability to force the outcome *Australia Collapse*. With Katich and Warne digging in, I therefore decide to go to bed, realising I've never once in my life gone to sleep certain that England will win a Test match. In fact, there are two sentences an English person should never utter:

'At least it's not raining.'

'Even England can't lose from here.'

Like believing in Father Christmas, I want to go to sleep and automatically have my life improve by the time I wake up. Hardly surprising, then, that I can't close my eyes. The cricket is on all night. This means that at any moment I can get up and check the score. Can't risk it. I lie in the dark, in bed, listening for waves and screeching car tyres.

Samuel Beckett, when he couldn't sleep, used to

imagine playing a round of golf on the old course at Carrickmines near Dublin, hole by hole. A biographer once asked him what then, Sam, what do you do then if you still can't sleep?

'I play the new course.'

I attempt the same remedy, setting myself up on the tee at Manly. I visualise my drive neatly bisecting the bunkers and trees on the first fairway, and select a three-wood, for safety. Slow back swing, eyes on the ball, controlled sweep down, slice my tee shot at right angles. This makes me more frantic than I was to start with. Then I can't find my ball.

Fourth Test, fifth day

There is no fifth day, because I wake up and Father Christmas has done what he does best. We won! It wasn't perfect (a three-wicket win, an almost disaster true to recent history) but at my age I'm not going to question Father Christmas – fat man thin chimney, so what's your point? I can now predict the future *and* I believe in Santa. This must be the broadening of the mind that travel always promised.

At Manly Library, first person through the doors, I eat up *The Telegraph, The Sydney Morning Herald, The Australian*. We won on the front and back pages of all of them, though there's no mention of my specific divine contribution. Every paper carries a picture of Adam Gilchrist, feet up on the Trent Bridge pavilion balcony. He appears to be crying, unmanned. There are calls to change everything, to change nothing. The players are too old, or too young. The leader writers and haggard ex-pros yearn for the good of the good old days.

This is like reading the papers in England, and as a reward for waking up bold and English and a thousand dollars richer, I treat myself with a trip to Manly Oceanworld. To get there, I stroll without cringing along the Manly Pathway of Olympians on West Esplanade Reserve. On the harbourside walkway turning left outside the ferry terminal, there is a pavement-level plaque for each of Manly's hundred Olympians, from 'Stan Rowley, 1900 Paris, Athletics', to 'Leonie Nichols, 2004 Athens, Synchronised Swimming'. I stop to pay my respects at 'Debbie Watson, 2000 Sydney, Gold Medal Water Polo'. Oh yes, I think, if only they could find more like Debbie to shore up their middle order.

Oceanworld, on the sheltered side of Manly, is the latest incarnation of the Manly Aquarium. Opened in 1886, this tourist attraction used to boast 'THE FINEST SEAL CAVERN IN THE WORLD' and 'THE BEST COLLECTION OF FISH AND SHARKS. IS THAT ALL? NO FEAR', as loud and confident as a bloodhouse drunk. They used to promise a fight between a shark and a seal three times its size, one or other of them (usually the shark) 'TORN TO SHREDS AND EATEN'. Such was entertainment before television.

Nothing so immediately compelling is offered in these enlightened times, but as well as sea life Oceanworld does have Dangerous Australian Animals, so on the back of England's victory I pay a visit to the five most venomous snakes in Australia. I'd have much preferred to see a death adder or a tiger snake sometime during the night in Ku-ring-gai Chase National Park, of course I would. I regret that outside my tent there wasn't a taipan to observe, or a cleverly camouflaged brown snake. If only I could have spotted in the wild, unprotected, a good example of the fierce snake, which has enough poison in one bite to kill nine teams of England cricketers. It wasn't as if I hadn't made the effort, but captive deadly snakes would just have to do.

The snakes are on the first floor in a row of five glass-fronted boxes. After tapping the glass and checking we're alone, I stand back and let the most toxic serpents on earth know what I think about them and their Australian danger now that England are 2–1 up in an Ashes series. 'Sheepshagger, la la la'. They're waking up and writhing against the glass, so I give them a dance and a taste of the second line – 'Sheepshagger, la la la'. And so on. Who's cringing now?

The Test victory still dissolving in my blood, I skip cheerfully downstairs into the submerged oceanarium. I now have water on both sides of me and overhead stingrays. It's a weekday afternoon in the winter season, so I'm alone in this transparent underwater doughnut, walking monastic blue circles beside kindly and incurious sea turtles. Two young children run round from the opposite direction, and then their mum and dad, and even in the blue filter of aquarium light I know that man. In the same way I recognise sharks, though I've never seen one in real life, I recognise George Gregan, captain of the Australian rugby union team.

This is too generous, even for Australia. They hire out their elite sportsmen one at a time to selected zoos around the nation. *George Gregan, scrum-half, commonly found in Canberra but also throughout New South Wales. Feeds mainly on scraps and can be highly territorial and aggressive, especially towards bigger fish. Max length 5′ 9″*.

I circle one way, they circle the other, just me, the George Gregan family, and overhead fish in the underworld blue of Manly's aerated Oceanworld. He must know I know who he is, but every time we cross I try not to stare. This is partly because I like to think I'm a discreet and thoughtful human being, and George Gregan is on an outing with his family just days after being stomped by the Boks in Pretoria. It's also because if he knows I know, which he must, he'll also know I'm being discreet and thoughtful, and that means he'll respect me as a human being, invite me to his house to have tea with the family, open a bottle of wine, ask me to be godfather to his younger child, and then confirm to a calling journalist that only the intervention of an English stranger opened his eyes to the inhumanity of loaning top sports achievers to Manly Oceanworld.

'I was just another exhibit,' said George, free at last to speak out. 'It was like living my life in a goldfish bowl.'

Fifth Test

The England cricket team need a draw to keep the Ashes at Lord's, which are kept at Lord's in any case. Much more importantly, they need a draw to win the series to banish the Cringe. The smart money, sweating beneath its specs, is still far too clever to speak for England. 'Please,' it insists, staring without blinking, 'don't insult my intelligence.' It stacks itself on the safe Australian side of the scales, trusting in reason and recent form and the fixed English habit of cringing. England are at 4.1 times the dollar to win. This is an insult, a kind of sneering financial sledge.

Since the second Test I've had A$200 on an England series victory. I add the usual A$200 on a match win, A$50 on Vaughan, A$50 on Harmison, and because everyone needs encouragement, A$50 on Geraint Jones not to drop a catch. This is perhaps getting out of hand, and when in the Australian first innings both openers reach a hundred, I gently remind God of my donation to Nic and the Christian Surfers. I then pray for rain, and God is not indifferent because all Sunday afternoon, just when the need is greater than ever for *Rain Saves England*, it rains heavily.

In Manly. After months of sunshine. How droll.

Back in London at the Oval we have to save ourselves, and a person ought to feel something seeing Andrew Flintoff on the fourth day of the last Test, charging in giving it one last barnyard howl. This is not a man given to cringing, and in this series, the excitement of players and fans alike has made amends for years of inferiority. The quest for heroes has, for once, been satisfied. Australian dominance was the problem. Freddie Flintoff is the solution.

I think we might actually do it. After half a lifetime of believing that Australians, simply because they're Australian, can outrun and outjump us, outhit and out-bowl us, the final Monday of the series offers a radical alternative. We can match them, beat them, if only we survive this single day at the crease. One day, just this one day, to fly in the face of *England Collapse*.

Even God occasionally gets bored with the idea of English sporting decline. On the final day of a twenty-five-day series the Ashes are saved by Kevin Pietersen, so conspicuously heaven's gift that he isn't even English. When he hits a four for his hundred he punches the air, I punch the air, we all do, and hours later, after the champagne and the medals and the celebrations, after the closing up of the deserted Steyne Hotel, I'm still raring to go. I have been released from the Cringe.

I bumble around Manly in the dark, alert and wide-eyed, listening to Australia silenced. Nothing stirs at the Oval, the golf course is empty, the swimming pool is locked. It's a funeral. The Fishos has nothing to show but torn posters for last week's live music. At the North Manly Bowls Club the rinks lie ashen in the moonlight, as deserted and mute as the art gallery and Oceanworld and the unlit window of Desire Books. All is shocked and still, a nation in grief at the loss of the Ashes: I can tightrope down the centre white lines of Pittwater Road.

As England rejoices, the Australians hide away. This is because the Cringe has come to an end. It's also because it's five o'clock in the morning.

A Tuesday morning, so not quite everyone in Manly is asleep. Billy and Maria are stretching and laughing on the dark promenade in front of the lifesaving club. Mona is with them.

'Mate!' Billy says. 'Comin' running?'

It's a kind of challenge, and I consider it in the absence of the Cringe, at last allowing for a considered and reasonable response.

'Billy,' I say. 'You know what? I'll meet you at the café when you get back.'

The flat paleness of the beach and then the white volleyball posts creep from the breaking light. An early surfer runs and splashes into the waves, launches himself face down onto his board, then paddles out and sits and waits. The sun is as patient, holding back for the perfect cloud bank, and then rises, carving out rays over the Pacific of Bible proportions.

This is the end of the Cringe. I and the gods and God and the England cricketers decree that enough is finally enough.

Whitewash

During all the years I have edited Wisden there has never been a season so disheartening . . . England was not merely beaten but overwhelmed.

S.H. Pardon, *Wisden*, 1921

Until the next time.

Partly I blame myself. While I was taking on the Australians in Manly the green and gold had a shocking winter's sport. In rugby league they lost the Tri-Nations title to New Zealand, while in union they tumbled along in their worst losing streak for thirty-six years. England gave them what for in the Ashes, and although 60,000 people turned out in Sydney to jog to Bondi Beach, one bronze medal was the haul from that July's 2005 World Athletics Championship.

I humbly accept responsibility for my small part in *Australia Collapse*, though I wouldn't want to brag. There was once a fashion for boys' adventure stories that depicted Australia as a barbarous and foreign land. It was the periphery, to be overcome by heroes travelling from the civilised European centre. That's not how it worked out for me, not exactly, even though I beat the Australians at every time of asking, at everything.

Nearly. I admit I lost to Frank at bowls, but he's English, so that doesn't count. Otherwise, although the scorecard might record that I didn't come first, results need to be adjusted using a retrospective calculation of my handicap. In every contest I had with an Australian I was playing off a lifetime of bad weather, too much reading, not enough steak and twenty years of England failing by example. On that handicap, I can hardly lose.

What a result. I'd set out on a mission, the most manly of sporting pursuits – challenging and beating the Australians – and I'd succeeded on my own, single-handed, every match an away fixture in any sport they cared to suggest. And what about the Ashes, eh?

I'd stemmed the tide, changed the course of England's sporting history, and from now on we could look forward to a more balanced rivalry in which sometimes one team won, and sometimes the other. It wouldn't be Australia against England as we knew it at all.

Or so I thought at the time. In Manly the virtue of telling things straight was often recommended. Best to avoid the unmanliness of tact and diplomacy, those evasive strategies that lead to European war and Gallipoli. So then, telling it straight, when it comes to the Ashes series of 2006/7: Rock Bottom. On my universal quality scale England quivered, barely registering, somewhere between the hard places of Utterly Embarrassing and Please Come Home.

I hold up my hands – I was no longer embedded in Manly, undermining the Australian effort. I made the basic English mistake of letting up. Said goodbye, went home, enjoyed the glow of victory and relived it in detail through my children, who are all going to play for England. I don't even have to get fit for that.

A mistake. Should have emigrated permanently, kept up the good work, lived a tough life undercover for the sake of all England. At the very least, come 2006, I should have placed some improbably optimistic bets. I didn't; the English cricketers somehow *knew*, and lost heart. It was as if I and many others had been secretly turned by the money, which again was stubbornly in Australia's favour. And this time it was right. Of course it was, because if it wasn't smart it wouldn't be money.

In short, despite the heroics of 2005, I was back where I belonged, behind the sofa. I couldn't watch / not watch / hated watching but somehow sofas aren't as broad-backed as they used to be, or the horror became so enveloping it seeped around the sides. Off with Sky (Atherton poised over the wreckage) and on with the computer to follow Cricinfo's less distressing procession of ball-by-ball numbers and Ws. There should have been something distancing and inhuman about cricket as dots and digits, that's what I'd hoped, a virtual humiliation less shattering than real English batsmen and bowlers toyed with and destroyed in Brisbane, Adelaide, Perth, Melbourne, Sydney. There were no exceptions, and reality refused to detach. The dropped catches, the mad-rabbit run-outs, the fear in the eyes; I didn't need to see them again because I'd seen them all before.

The Cringe was back.

That and sleep deprivation made every morning a hangover, to the point where I couldn't see straight when searching my bookshelves for the DVD of *2005 The Greatest Series*. The sleepless Cringe could provoke such unfocused misery that my weary Cricinfo eyes roamed the shelves reading every 'English' as 'Rubbish'. Where was that blessed DVD? I passed over W.G. Hoskins's classic *The Making of the Rubbish Landscape*; *Rubbish Journey* by J.B. Priestley, and then the lesser-known *Domestic Interiors: The Rubbish Tradition 1500–1850*. Until finally, just beyond *Rubbish Garden Birds*, I spotted the shine of the plastic-backed DVD box set.

I took it out and sat down. Not to watch it, just to hold it close to my heart. Oh such tender melancholy. It was true then; we did once beat the Australians, because Vaughan is forever on the cover gurning with the urn, enjoying the bright burn of once having been the best. Only hours earlier, in a time already receding.

From experience, representing the splinter of England that will always be me, I know that the English have a fierce will to win and try as hard as anyone on earth. The derision aimed at failing English sportspeople can therefore seem unkind, like the worst type of gossip. We all know the characters involved and everyone has an opinion (Did I mention Michael Atherton? And since when did angry Glenn McGrath become a role model?) but few of us are actually involved. We watch glitter-eyed from the outside, avid for happenings, judgemental, cruel. It's so easy for us – 'Bowl straight, for God's sake, on off stump!' I would. But they won't take advice, preferring leg-side half-volleys as the better option. They lose.

And after every loss there isn't one England supporter who doesn't know the secret of how to beat the Australians. My way. Listen in, learn; we have hours and the England middle order to kill before closing time.

Sadly, the day has yet to come when a barroom pundit is elected prime minister on the credible single-issue slate of beating the Australians. No individual gets to implement the cure or spend the money, and in the absence of such a benign despot we need first to stop and consider why the Australians are consistently superior.

Until the First World War, Australian sporting victories were explained away by the 'Englishness' of Australians. They won because they were just like us. Good show. Later, when this finesse became untenable, the Australians won because of their 'Australianness'. Along with grudging admiration for a kind of pioneer toughness, this definition included implicit disapproval of a nation so obsessed by winning that England could miss their turn. 'Australianness' was both a term of disparagement and a pretext for the sorry English habit of losing. The Australians won because they cared too much.

The limitation of this excuse, as anyone can discover by looking more closely, is that it's wrong. The Australians are no more obsessed by sport and winning than we are. This truth, unwelcome though it may be, can be established by spending a winter in a Sydney suburb going to readings, galleries and concerts. There is life beyond sport in the suburb of Manly, a fact confirmed in Manly Library by obscure academic works heavily reliant on statistics, so no one need ever know. However, testable comparisons have been made by respected doctors of sport, collating reliable data on participation, attendance and television coverage. The results show that Australia is as sports-minded and sports-active, but no more so, than many other countries. These include the United States, Brazil and Britain.

Between 2003 and 2005, in our nation less obsessed, London was brought to a standstill three times in honour of sporting heroes. You can wait decades for an open-top bus, and then three come along at once. Two of these celebrations, in rugby and cricket, were for victories over Australia. It was about time.

Not that I'd recommend the victory-parade business to enterprising sixth-form leavers. The Australians are back on top, but why should that be?

For Australians below the highest level, at my level, I can only speak for Manly. I know the tough western suburbs of Sydney exist, and the vast outback, and Melbourne, but Manly is where I was. Nor did I get a chance to play every sport the Australians play, even though each one has different implications politically, culturally and for the state of my knees. I missed out on team sports like football (right midfield, good engine). I didn't compete with Australians at netball or Australian Rules, or America's Cup. I wish I could have done. Perhaps one day I will.

What I do now appreciate is that Australians are good at sport because of the terms and conditions for licensed premises, and the special attraction of any kind of club in an immigrant society. The absence of class barriers and puritan guilt helps them to take sport seriously, while they're fit and ambitious because the non-sport television is appalling. In a small population fellow Australians who've achieved the dream live next door, or in the same street, and even at the humblest level points and positions are always recorded, the Australians are competitive because this is the way their sport is organised and organised this way because they're competitive. They're hard to beat because the council supports facilities that make it easy to walk round the corner and have a go, and they're reliably inspired by any of the forty-one sporting events saved by law for free-to-air broadcast. The beach is a physical challenge accessible to everyone, where schoolkids out for lunch bundle up their uniforms and sprint into the ocean, mini-Australians developing complex motor skills and disciplined muscle groups. The gold-rush mentality and immigrant energy make most sports worth a try (and worth trying harder with money on the nose). And then when Australians do eventually make it, the blunt closeness of the Hill at Brookie will remind them who they are and where they came from.

Yes, yes, but *apart* from that?

The weather.

All of which may help explain why we haven't seen the last of the Cringe.

The Australian sporting slump of 2005 was depressingly brief. Between losing the Ashes and grabbing them back, the cricket team didn't lose a Test. The Kangaroos reclaimed the Tri-Nations rugby league trophy, and an Australian freestyle skier won another of those unlikely gold medals at the Turin Winter Olympics (Britain no golds). Two Australian riders finished in the top ten of the Tour de France, and another claimed the sprinters' Green Jersey. Australians also won the Australian Rules Grand Final in front of 100,000 spectators in Melbourne, the one annual event at the MCG where Australians (half the crowd) go home disappointed.

That year's international multi-sport tournament, the Commonwealth Games, was also held in Melbourne. Australians won 84 gold medals, as many as England (36), Canada (26) and India (22) combined. This was too much for some of the competitors. A total of twenty-five athletes went missing, including two thirds of Sierra Leone's twenty-one-strong team, a Bangladeshi runner and a Tanzanian boxer. They'd seen enough. They couldn't beat the Australians so they obeyed the phrase and tried to join them. Six of Sierra Leone's sporting exiles, like so many random visitors before them, later turned up in Manly.

At the FIFA World Cup in Germany the Socceroos survived their group of death and lost narrowly in the round of sixteen to Italy, eventual world champions. (England? Football, cricket, whatever; we're beyond worrying about results. The way we prepare and perform suggests we're now more worried about worrying.)

On to the Gabba for the Ashes, where the Australians challenged the notion of cricket as a non-contact, physically aloof sport. Swiftly and without mercy they re-established the harshest assumptions of the last twenty years: they won because they were Australia and we lost because we were England, which was pretty much the unacceptable situation when I first came in. This can't be right. Something must be done. I believe I've said that before.

But what? What now? How to beat the Australians?

I ought to say I'm fond of the Rubbish Isles and Europe, and not that keen on solving the problem by permanent exile to Manly. Unless, that is, the situation deteriorates, and as any experienced supporter knows, with England it can always get worse. When your team falls off the edge of the world there is no rock bottom, and even though I've discovered that living in Manly works, I'm not yet prepared to move there permanently. I'm unwilling to make the sacrifice, to grunt up. I am English.

No one wants to believe that being English is the main problem with English sports teams. If it is, we can change. We can become more like Australians. This must be why in recent times our best idea of how to beat them amounts to copying their systems and structures as submissively as possible. Is this what Jesus would do?

I only ask because the Manly Christian surfers have waterproof wristbands with the reminder WWJD. English sports administrators have the same only less salty and inscribed with the letters WWAD: What would Australia do? Australian coaches now litter English sport, where we take their second-raters as they used to take our second-rate aristocrats, some of whom, though a minority, turned out to be first rate. We have Australian-style academies and central contracts, and we cloister and closet our young and strong amid the like-minded and machines that go bleep. Even the government has joined in, failing to meet its targets for the Kyoto Protocol and therefore doing what it can to improve the weather.

I wouldn't mind so much if we were genuinely prepared to duplicate those extreme Australian measures that make them the competitors they are today. It seems unlikely, however, that we'll ever manage to follow a precedent such as the State of Victoria's reaction to a cricket losing streak between 1856 and 1858. They realised they needed to toughen up over the winter months, so invented Australian Rules. This kind of energetic problem solving is the Victorian sporting value system as under-stood in Australia, even back in the days of imported Queen Victorian fair play and fatalism.

In 2007 we were also on a cricket losing streak. The ECB appointed a committee. The situation would be reviewed. Now, you might have thought that the shambolic Ashes tour had already proved that English cricket was full of losers. Not so. It seemed there was always room for more, and the ECB's Review Committee included six former Test cricketers not one of whom had contested a winning series against Australia. Nasser Hussein and Angus Fraser, great fighters as players, had between them an Ashes record of Played 35 Won 9 Drawn 7 Lost 19. This poor long-suffering pair were supposed to give credibility to the committee set up to find the answer of how to beat Australia. It might work.

At least the choice of chairman was inspired. Ken Schofield, a golfer with no experience in cricket, must have been the last man standing in British sport not yet traumatised by exposure to Australians. He helped Europe win the Ryder Cup, no Australians involved.

The committee, I imagine, will have consulted those home-grown coaches, horribly few, who know what it's like to win against Australia. Been there, done that, if not every time then at least occasionally. Clive Woodward, never knowingly shy about his contribution to England's victory in the Rugby World Cup, tells us in his book *Winning!* that 'we have managed to stem the tide and change the course of England's sporting history'. You too?

For precisely 81 minutes. In cricket, we managed to hold the Ashes for 272 days, the shortest period on record, and England's sporting history refuses to deviate. Having said that, the 2006/7 tourists did carefully extract the madness from Woodward's method, and decided a bloated back-up staff and full-time security guards were just what a cricket team needs.

Any combination of pampering and pathetic capitulation inevitably leads, as with our footballers, to criticism that England's elite performers are overprotected. They're cushioned from the fans, from reality, from the hard sidelines that make victory sweet. Even on the road they have their wives and families and tickets to Kylie Minogue. But then cosseting was also a Woodward innovation, one which reached its endgame on his feeble Lions' tour to New Zealand, when on a chartered inland flight the headrest covers were embroidered with each player's initials. The theory is that if you treat the players as special then that's how they'll play.

It's not a bad idea, but the other extreme is Mike Tyson doing away with frills altogether and stepping into the ring in 1986 without socks, without hair, in black, as unbeatable a proposition as any in sport (until he was beaten). The skill is to decide on the right approach with the right people at the right time. Boot camps or the VIP enclosure at Elton John. You decide (but don't ask the players).

In either case, the main task of beating the Australians can ultimately be achieved only by confronting the look – the narrowed eyes, the gunslinger squint, the thinned lips. The look was out in force on the face of Cricket Australia in the winter they regained the Ashes. Vietnam veterans have the thousand-mile stare, but the Australian cricketers were more focused than that, the stare beamed in unblinking at twenty-two yards. All Australian sportsmen have it, or learn it, or grow it. It's an expression chiselled by years outside in the sunshine, a creased determination, a tunnel vision that excludes any peripheral flicker of doubt or self-destruction.

Ricky Ponting has become a study in the look, a recognisable model in a line of narrow-eyed, low-peaked, will-to-win Australia cricket captains. For Ponting see Steve Waugh, Allan Border, Ian Chappell, Richie Benaud, these and many others hard and sly in the baggy green shadow.

Challenging the look is never easy, but if we can do that, then an Australian sportsman may falter. We need to remember or invent some English strategies for making that Australian stare waver, not imitate the Australian way of winning. They know how their own method works. They invented it and they're better at it. If we insist on copying, we'll carry on losing. Start near the back. Exaggerate your handicap. Surprise them.

Perhaps we'll carry on losing anyway, whatever approach we take, whatever the sport; Twenty20 cricket was a fine example of English inventiveness, and our northern hemisphere supremacy lasted one whole match. By the second international Australia had worked it out, but at least inventing new games shows a bit of creative fight. Sport in England is a broad church, always has been, extending far beyond today's professional flagship sports. It takes the sixteenth-century antiquarian John Stow, for example, to put football and cricket back in their original perspective, among the many other pastimes available at the beginning of English time: 'the more common sort divert themselves at Football, Wrestling, Cudgels, Nine-pins, Shovelboard, Cricket, Stowball, Ringing of Bells, Quoits, pitching the bar, Bull and Bear baiting, throwing at cocks, and lying at alehouses'.

There's more to sport against Australia than the Ashes, and ours is the larger population. The more sports we play, the thinner Australian talent gets spread. Perhaps that's the answer. Come and try us at bell-ringing (if you think you're hard enough). Though, let's face it, no one in England would honestly be surprised if Sky Sports 3 broadcast competitive international bell-ringing and the Australians brought the look to Canterbury Cathedral and trounced us. I already believe rumours that the English captain crumbled under well-aimed sledging. Call that a dong?

I tell myself, sometimes, we don't need to do anything at all. Sporting success goes in cycles and better days will come around. The last time England lost an Ashes series 5–0 was in 1920/1, when the captain was the same J.W.H.T. Douglas knocked cold at the National Sporting Club by Snowy Baker. On that occasion the editor of *Wisden*, Sydney Pardon, bemoaned the worst season ever in all known human history, as infallibly recorded by the biblical yellow brick. Sydney Pardon was mistaken. We've now seen a worse season, but between the two barrel bottoms there were many outdoor summers in the sun. If we wait, we will rise again, and like Pardon see England prevail once more through brutal premeditated cheating (Bodyline) or individual genius-heroes like Denis Compton, Ian Botham, Freddie Flintoff.

Australia against England is the world's oldest international sporting rivalry. In one lifetime we see only episodes, get dispirited by events which are a small part of a broader narrative. Like all epics the story is long, keeps changing and attracts the indulgence of the gods. Australia won the first ever Test match, at the MCG in 1877 by 45 runs. A hundred years later on the same ground Australia won the Centenary Test by an identical margin, 45 runs. The planets were aligned, the yin and yang in balance, the mythical dimension confirmed. This is legendary territory, and not even Achilles wins for ever.

As for me, I wanted to play some part before it was too late, because traditions change weight and ancient contests fade. In cricket the match between Oxford and Cambridge used to be second only to Eton versus Harrow as a gala outing at Lord's. Some people still care deeply about who wins, but not many, and the same fate awaits England against Australia. We should celebrate the rivalry, and the emotion that comes with winning and losing, but we shouldn't imagine it will always matter.

Every sport codified by the British has had to endure the same awkward rite of passage. First establish a club. Use 'All-England' in the title and find a tame aristocrat to promote the colours on his cummerbund. Rules should then be agreed and minuted at a London club by practical men in deep leather armchairs. Now hold an open competitive championship closed to women and professionals. This is a misjudgement. We should also have excluded foreigners, who before too long are winning the All-England trophies.

In cricket and tennis and rugby, in bowls and rowing and swimming, Australian victories were an inconsiderately early and therefore painful phase of this process. Australians beat us first and have beaten us most often and consistently since, but insisting on the historic connection seems blinkered now that England is playing against a country with 120 ethnic groups, 90 languages, 60 religions, Gerry Muio and Maria Silva.

Australians care about sport, as do we. Out of vanity, we hope they care most about sport against the old enemy, the Poms, but in a ranking of Australian national sports by participation, none of the top five – golf, basketball, Australian Rules, netball, soccer – are sports with a strong traditional rivalry with England. This may explain why we like it when warning signs go up on Manly Beach, days before the 2003 Rugby World Cup final, proclaiming *Caution: Boring Rugby Team Trains Here*. They're looking at us. They're paying attention. There was a kind of reassurance in the ferocious verve the Australians brought to the task of winning back the Ashes. It was a compliment, because the English aren't as important in Australia as they used to be, and sport is a sentimental connection occasionally overvalued precisely because it's fading.

The Australian public are interested, sure, because the British are still the largest group in the 23 per cent of Australians born abroad, 6 per cent of the total population. But they're now one minority among many, with no privileged status or claim on the core identity of contemporary Australia. Some Australians don't like this fact, but many of them will soon be dying of heart disease from drinking too much beer on hot Sunday mornings at winter swimming clubs while fretting about Arabs and intermittent campaigns for a new national flag. My own idea is to shrink the Union Jack in the corner of the existing Australian flag by half a centimetre each year. No one will notice, and in twenty years it'll be gone.

This would reflect a process already well under way. SBS (Special Broadcasting Service) is the terrestrial channel that broadcast the most recent Ashes series from England. When there's no cricket from abroad, SBS is an ethnic channel which offers morning news in Hungarian, Maltese, Polish and Ukrainian – without subtitles. It is the 'voice and vision of multicultural Australia', and cricket from England is one proud element of that tradition. One among many. To English immigrants and Australians who like cricket, the Ashes has an ethnic appeal. The presenter, a man named Simon Hill, is ethnically English, in the same way that SBS would want an ethnic Italian to front broadcasts of top-line *bocce*.

Australia is already living a future divorced from its British past. Where once sporting victories over England could help unify the nation, these days the Olympics and FIFA World Cups – sports in which Australia can compete with the rest of the world – are better candidates for the same job. The traditional duel with England was largely irrelevant when in 2006, in front of a worldwide TV audience of a hundred million, the Socceroos in green and gold ran out for their first World Cup Finals appearance in thirty years. They were up against Asian neighbour and economic competitor Japan. Later in the tournament they battled with Croatia and Italy, new rivalries bred from more recent patterns of immigration.

There was no sense of disappointment or frustration that these opponents failed to live up to history and past glories. No one condescended to suggest that these nations were spent and couldn't give Australia a game.

We might, from time to time, distract ourselves from our own urgent misery to celebrate Australian achievements. If their national talent for sport is a kind of genius, that would partly explain why it's hard to account for. We could allow that Australians have some special feel and affinity for physical activity of many kinds, just as the German-speaking peoples once had for music. We cringe before them as bested opponents, but we might also enjoy the quality, be grateful for images of Australian brilliance among the satellite junk in every modern head – Kathy Freeman's 400 metres or Ricky Ponting's pull shot in permanent orbit, occasionally visible from humble planet earth. They offer glimpses of human potential.

These Australian champions embody a personality type unfamiliar to us, outside our standard experience, as if even now we find it hard to accept that Australian sport is its own distinct culture and not a dependency of ours. Gone are the days of Robert Menzies, the anglophile Australian prime minister who allowed the atomic-bombing of the outback before an agreeable stint as president of Kent County Cricket Club. It's a very long time since different kettle, same fish.

That explains why the Liberate Saturday Nights from Sport Association was destined to fail. It was an anti-movement, when in Manly a pro-movement was always more likely to get popular backing. This is a much bigger difference between England and Australia than how good or bad we are at sport. We have major political parties that are anti-movements; they have a positivism that reaches far beyond the playing field, to mission Christianity to arts festivals and coffee on the beach. It's just that until recently sport, in particular international sport, has been more visible.

Elite sport is an unforgiving win–lose equation. This tends to mean that English inquests into differences on the games field can curdle into a perception of more general deficiencies. We're made to wrestle earnestly with the knot of what 'English' means, a conundrum that royally vexes us when elsewhere in the world this word has a clear and fixed meaning, agreed internationally. It's a certain type of breakfast.

As for the Australians, it's worth looking at what D.H. Lawrence took away from Manly after his visit in the 1920s. He stole some house names to use in *Kangaroo*. Wyewurk was one, and another was The Better 'Ole, after the famous First World War cartoon of two glum-looking Tommies in a shell hole on the Western Front: 'Well if you knows of a better 'ole, go to it.'

Some time in the recent experience of every Australian family, they heard of a better hole. They went to it. They have the gift of picking themselves up and starting afresh, a talent for recreation, and Australian government research in the 1950s found that successful applicants for immigration were more likely to have 'energetic, outgoing personalities'. These types of people could be recognised by giving the impression 'they felt themselves to be more in charge of their destinies and less the pawns of fate than did the non-emigrants'.

Or in other words, successful immigrants have a winning mentality. This at least offers hope that from now on England will not always be collapsing. The collective will to define ourselves through sport may once have come and gone, but it could feasibly return to a new incarnation of Britain, modern and multicultural, not so dissimilar to Australia. This is a more likely source of sporting revitalisation than a doomed quest for former glories, meaning certainties – the grandparents of Monty Panesar did not send the grandparents of Andrew Symonds to Botany Bay.

We have grown apart like different religious sects. We pay homage to the same monotheist god, sporting success, but whereas the Australians are the active branch of the belief we're mostly contemplative. They love to do it and we love to think about it, and talk about it. After the event we do a cracking illuminated manuscript, full of debate about Team England and what it says about who we are. We study the players for any particular quality that reflects us back to ourselves, and recently we've seen most often in the mirror the uncertain poke, the hang of the head, the gloves in the helmet and long trudge home.

That can't be right. Something must be done. Fortunately, this reaction is also part of the reflection.

Acknowledgements

I would like to thank everyone in Manly who helped out during my visit to Australia. Most of these people are in the book, and I won't repeat myself by thanking each of them again individually here. Except for Maria Silva, who was and remains unfailingly cheerful and cooperative.

For invaluable advice and welcome encouragement, I'm significantly indebted to John MacRitchie, Local Studies Librarian at Manly Library. He found me everything I needed, however fanciful, generously answered all my follow-up questions and kindly read through an early draft of this book, though of course any errors that remain are mine alone.

In Japan, I particularly appreciate the friendship of Professor Shiro Yamamoto and novelist Clive Collins, who between them have made Tokyo University an invigorating place to be writing this book; in London I'm grateful for Tristan Jones, my expert tailor at Yellow Jersey, and for the unstinting guidance and support of Zoe Waldie at Rogers, Coleridge and White.

Most of all I owe a debt to Laurence, for this and many other adventures.